MOUNTED

ON HORSES, BLACKNESS, AND LIBERATION

MOUNTED

BITTER KALLI

AMISTAD

An Imprint of HarperCollins*Publishers*

FIRST EDITION

Designed by Kyle O'Brien

Artwork on page iii courtesy of the Artist, Jack Shainman Gallery, New York, and Various Small Fires, Los Angeles / Texas / Seoul

Library of Congress Cataloging-in-Publication Data has been applied for.

ISBN 978-0-06-337175-0

25 26 27 28 29 LBC 5 4 3 2 1

CONTENTS

CONTENTS

INTRODUCTION

In 2015, the *Los Angeles Times* tweeted side-by-side images of Serena Williams and racehorse American Pharoah along with the question "Who's the real sportsperson of 2015?" The tweet referenced the Sports Illustrated Sportsperson of the Year title, which Williams and American Pharoah had both contended for. Williams had won, but public dissatisfaction continued, with the horse's jockey describing the title as a "sham." As many online critics noted, there were clear racial undertones in the comparisons between Williams and American Pharoah. *Sports Illustrated* readers had voted for the horse over Williams, and many simply seemed resentful of a Black woman athlete winning the title. The controversy followed years of similarly racist commentary; over the course of her career, audiences and viewers routinely assigned animalistic qualities to Williams when describing her physical prowess and strength. This wasn't the first time a Black athlete had been compared to a horse or even made to compete against one. Throughout American history, the relationship between horses and Black people has become a singular site for complex negotiations around labor, racial hierarchy, and white anxieties.

In the fall of 2014, I was marching through New York City with my classmates to protest the police killing of a Black man named Michael Brown. Later, from the common room of my college dorm, I watched footage of protests in Ferguson, Missouri, where Brown had been killed. I was struck by the images of walls of mounted police officers facing down unarmed protesters, guns and batons at the ready.

I was seventeen years old and had recently moved from the largely Black, rapidly gentrifying Brooklyn neighborhood where I was raised to a predominantly white campus uptown. I had learned to ride horses as a child at Brooklyn's Kensington Stables, a small, racially diverse urban stable located across the street from Prospect Park. After riding throughout high school, I had joined my college's equestrian team weeks after Michael Brown was shot on a Ferguson street. That night in my dorm, I wondered what I would see in those horses' eyes if I were one of the protesters in Missouri. I wondered if their gazes would feel at all familiar, or if I would see only my reflection staring back at me in the polished surfaces of the police shields.

This book explores many of the tensions I was beginning to understand in that moment of protest and personal change. In these essays, I examine some of the relationships between Blackness and horses, exploring what these connections can teach us about nationhood, race, and American landscapes both mythical and physical. From mounted cops and Border Patrol agents to equestrian-influenced fashion trends, from Lil Nas X's "Old Town Road" to public statues of Civil War generals on horseback, horses are ubiquitous in American cultural and political life. Obviously, these phenomena are not equivalent when it comes to their material impact on everyday life. In terms of their effect on people's ability to survive, the influence of officers who enforce US border policy is worlds away from the influence of a statue in a city park. In engaging with such a wide range of examples, I show how the horse operates on multiple levels of society, from the media we encounter every day to the economic structures underlying our lives.

Equestrian sports in the Western world originated with and evolved alongside militarization. Until the 1952 Olympic Games in Helsinki, only military officers were allowed to compete on the United States Olympic equestrian team. Much of the apparel, training customs, and techniques of equestrian sports are drawn from a history of military conquest, and therefore from a history of colonial domination. What does it mean, then, for Black people to ride and tend horses within a context where horses are also used as tools of terror against them?

I was the only Black member of the equestrian team in college, and the one who could least afford the activity. In order to offset my costs, I took on administrative work for the team in addition to my campus job. My coach still ended up threatening me with legal action over a few hundred dollars of late lesson fees. Over my two years on the team, I began reckoning with the tenuous relationship between Blackness and mainstream equestrian sports, the dissonance I often felt when I considered how I carried my body, my gender, my histories, through the overwhelming elitism and whiteness of the horse world that I knew.

In early 2015, protesters took to the streets again over the killing of Freddie Gray, just months after we'd been chanting Michael Brown's name. The immediacy and rage of the protests—where we moved like a single grieving body through the choked freeways and avenues of the city—felt irreconcilably distant from the suburban New Jersey barn where I went for team practice. My teammates and I never discussed race or the protests happening outside the gates of our campus. In order to be an equestrian in that space, I had to sever parts of myself from one another.

I first began writing this book in college, although I didn't know it then. The earliest thing I remember writing for this project was an angsty Tumblr post about being on the equestrian team and wanting to learn more about the history of Black and brown people riding horses. In the post, I recalled a conversation I'd had with my friend about how much I loved horses and how disconnected I felt from the culture and values of the team. My friend told me that when her mom was a young girl in southern China, having a horse meant you could travel farther to dig up potatoes for food. I had been complaining about what the horse represented in a WASPy, Northeastern US context, but my friend helped me remember the tangible role of horses in people's lives, the ways that horses exist beyond just being a symbol of status and power. It's a lesson I have tried to keep close throughout the process of writing this book, as I've explored the ways horses have been intertwined with the urgency of survival and the creativity of self-making— from all-Black rodeos and Reconstruction-era farming to BDSM practices and diasporic religious traditions.

While many of this project's early preoccupations emerged during college and my time on the equestrian team, I'm wary of playing into the mythical image of the Only Black Person. Too often, such experiences are presented as proof of exceptionalism, with the unspoken implication being that if you are the only Black or brown person in a sea of whiteness, you were somehow good enough to make it, to distinguish yourself from all the others like you. But as Elaine Castillo writes in *How to Read Now*, being "the only" in a white space is as much a marker of access as it is an indicator of social alienation. I grew up in a lower-middle-class family in Brooklyn, and my parents invested large amounts of time and money into me and my sister's education. My homeschooled childhood was characterized by the kinds of near-comical contrasts one might find in a family whose adjacency to cultural capital far outweighs their financial capital. While my family of four lived in a cluttered one-bedroom apartment until I was seventeen, my sister and I, through a combination of financial aid, scholarships, and debt, participated in the kinds of activities often seen as belonging to people who were wealthier and whiter than us. Some of this was the result of growing up in a city where—despite staggering levels of school segregation and economic disparity—philanthropic wealth has created some well-funded pathways to make things like classical music nominally more accessible to children.

Still: we came home from a horseback riding lesson to a 550-square-foot apartment. Our parents struggled to pay the bills, but we practiced music in our tiny kitchen and played in orchestras. And for most of elementary school, I could name an opera singer more readily than I could a Nickelodeon show or pop star (a relationship to popular culture I am still trying to remedy). In different ways, my parents wanted us to be exposed to things they couldn't access in their own childhoods. Intentionally or not, this also meant I was primed to participate in the myth of exceptionalism peddled by a racist educational system. By the time I joined the equestrian team, I was well practiced in making myself palatable to white institutions, even though I was critically aware of their shortcomings.

The deeper I ventured into the project of *Mounted*, the more it demanded I challenge the individualist beliefs that surrounded me, the ideologies that I had in some ways internalized too. The yearning I described in that Tumblr post was not a desire for individual recognition, but for seeing myself as part of a collective. I was asking questions about a lineage. As I attempted to answer these questions, I found urban cowboys, Jamaican dancehall DJs, and fictional pony girls. I found Brooklyn youth creating new fashion idioms, and mounted protesters walking their horses through the streets of Houston and Los Angeles. I learned from countless examples of Black people interacting with horses in ways that were about plotting escape routes, distributing resources to their communities, and making art that illuminated the complex geographies of displacement and empire.

Much has changed in the world, and in myself, since I wrote the first few blog posts and essays that would become this book. On a personal level, realizing I was trans helped clarify some things about my relationship to embodiment, and to archetypes like the Pony Girl. Over the years, I have also deepened my knowledge about spiritual and ecological traditions throughout the African diaspora, leading me to understand the relationship between Black people and horses as one that both predates chattel slavery and is inextricable from practices of the sacred. On a larger scale, the first Donald Trump presidency and the COVID-19 pandemic made even clearer the ways that capitalism has created conditions of intentional neglect and avoidable mass death. In October 2023, Israel began its siege on Palestine's Gaza Strip. As this book goes to press, the official (almost certainly underreported) death toll of Palestinians killed in the war has surpassed 42,000. Witnessing this brutal chapter in the Palestinian genocide, alongside the worldwide rallies, marches, and educational efforts aiming to bring it to a halt, has impacted my thinking about protest and collective action. Palestine has challenged me to be more attentive to the why and how of political resistance efforts, and—in craft as well as life—to resist learned tendencies toward the vague and the figurative when describing the very tangible processes of settler colonialism, imperialism, and ecological devastation.

Looking at the intertwined histories and present of Black people and horses reminds us that dismantling oppressive systems isn't just about humans. It's about all the forms of life and landscape entangled within those systems. The practices Black people have established with horses address fundamental questions of our political moment: How do we create generative and resilient relationships despite and beyond the ever-present terror of state violence? How can we organize, come together, and support the transfer of knowledge while capitalism seeks to alienate us and keep us isolated from one another? In a time of increasing climate destruction, genocide, and global health crisis, when calls for systemic change feel ever more urgent, the relationships between Black people and horses hold crucial lessons about creating a world free of dispossession.

FUGITIVITY

*These Negroes took with them a bright bay Horse, nearly
five Feet high, five Years old this Spring. . . . Any person
apprehending either of the said Negroes, and restores
him to his Owner, will receive Twenty Dollars Reward;
or Forty-five Dollars for both the Negroes and the Horses.*

—Wm. [William] Mitchell and Wilson Jones,
Raleigh Register and North Carolina Weekly Advertiser,
March 25, 1801

The first time I met the horses and the fugitives, I
wanted to speak with them directly. I wanted to
know them better, to hear how they planned their escapes,
what the moon looked like on the night they left, how they
said their farewells. Sometimes they answered, but most
of the time they were already riding out of reach.

In the century before slavery was abolished in the United States, advertisements for escaped slaves were regularly printed in newspapers throughout the country. Often, these ads were not only for the people who had run away, but also for the horses they had taken with them. In the ads, slaveholders offered rewards for their lost property—twenty dollars, seventy dollars, forty-five, sometimes more for the horse than the person. The ads listed physical descriptions of the runaways and the horses; many of them carried the marks of plantation labor on their bodies.

They were jockeys, plowers, wagon drivers, carpenters, printing press operators, shoemakers, barbers, cockfighters, coopers, bricklayers, and painters. They were regular old negroes described as having no particular skills save for shiftiness and connivance. They had burns and scars on their faces, they had unusually small eyes, they had scars on their wrists and knees, they had bowlegs, they were around five feet ten, they had bushy heads, they were stout, they were slender and stately, they were six feet tall. They stole horses.

I don't want to romanticize the horses. It's likely that many of the people in the escaped slave notices saw their relationships with horses as mainly one of convenience or necessity. Horses were a mode of transportation, a way of moving quickly across vast distances. But in many ways, it's the unremarkable nature of this relationship that draws me to these stories.

Horses were a part of the daily fabric of life for many enslaved Black people. The work done by horses, and the enslaved Black people who cared for and maintained the horses, was central to the social and economic landscape of the plantation South. On the plantation, horses pulled plows and other heavy machinery and cultivated miles of cash crops. They provided the primary means of transit on and between plantations and neighboring towns, transporting wagons and carrying riders on their backs, sometimes for multiple-day journeys. Enslaved Black people performed the daily work of grooming, exercising, saddling, and feeding horses. Here, as elsewhere, Black people were responsible for maintaining life—of slaveholders' families, of agricultural animals like mules, oxen, and horses—even as they were denied the conditions to nurture their own survival.

The escaped slaves who stole horses were exercising the genius of fugitivity: using the mundane to achieve the extraordinary, looking at the resources available and imagining new uses, resistive relations. Stealing horses was an act that shattered the illusion of plantation owners' control over their land and property. It intervened in the set of circumscribed relationships between Black people, agricultural animals, and white slaveholders that had been established under slavery. For an escaping slave to steal a horse—property stealing property—posed an economic threat to the plantation. This is why, in the newspaper ads, plantation owners were eager to get their horses back even without the enslaved person who stole them. It's better to lose one laborer than two.

*   *   *

In 1872, Philadelphia abolitionist William Still published *The Underground Railroad Records*, a massive collection of letters, firsthand accounts, and transcribed stories of the experiences of Black people who escaped slavery. Here, too, were the horses transporting escaping slaves across rivers, pulling them in carriages, carrying them to the next stop on the railroad.

In 1856, Owen Taylor escaped from Maryland with his wife, child, and two brothers. They were received by the abolitionists of the Philadelphia Vigilance Committee. As Still writes, the Taylors had determined that if slave catchers caught up to them, "somebody would have to bite the dust. That they had pledged themselves never to surrender alive, was obvious." Still was struck by the closeness and care shown among the group, "the joy that the tokens of friendship afforded them."

"Never to surrender alive." In making this promise to fight to the death, this acknowledgment of the ways mortality was hastened for so many Black people, the Taylors were also promising to remember the gravity of what it meant to be alive and free. These ancestors whisper through the archives that they were not content to live a half life, and that even under the unrelenting violence of our world, neither should we.

Still titles the chapter about the Taylors "Owen and Otho Taylor's Flight with Horses, etc." Setting out from the plantation, the Taylors stole two horses from their master, Mr. Fiery. The horses pulled the Taylor brothers' wives and children in a carriage, with a speed "that allowed no grass to grow under the horses' feet." When they reached Pennsylvania, they "bade their faithful beasts goodbye" and continued on in carriages. I imagine whispered farewells, a firm pat on a horse's nose or shoulder before moving on to the next stage of the journey. Or maybe there was no time for all of that, just a glance in the direction of a stable as it receded into the distance.

The Taylors reached freedom in Canada despite Mr. Fiery's repeated letters attempting to bribe them back into slavery. From Canada, Otho often wrote Still asking for help getting his enslaved family members from Maryland. Still writes that the dangers of such journeys and the abolitionists' limited funds meant no assistance could be given to Otho. It is here that the story—as much of it as we know from Still's accounting—comes to an end.

It could be argued that horses were also natural accessories to escape. In addition to speed, they conferred the gift of secrecy. In the Taylors' story, Still writes, "The horses were easily captured at the hotel, where they were left, but, of course, they were mute as to what had become of their drivers." Even if stolen horses were found and returned to the plantation owners, they could not communicate where they had been, or what they had seen.

★   ★   ★

In 1822, a slaveholder posted a notice in Newbern, North Carolina, in the *Carolina Sentinel*, with a reward for the capture of an enslaved person named London Pollock. He described London as a house servant who was "very fond of dress" and who had left wearing a coat with "velvet collar . . . and striped pantaloons." London had stolen a horse, who wore "a saddle and bridle with plated mountings." Unlike many of the other advertisements, this one doesn't mention a separate reward for the horse. Instead, it highlights London's flamboyance and describes him as an "uncommonly intelligent and likely boy." London's theft of a horse became part of a larger narrative of being flashy, ostentatious, too smart for his own good. I'm thinking about the material of fugitivity, its weight and heft. The cloth and leather and striped pantaloons that go into the fashioning of escape.

★　　★　　★

On October 4, 1842, a Black man named Hardy Carroll escaped from the Broke Wake County Jail in Raleigh, North Carolina. Carroll, described in the paper as a "dark complected free negro," had escaped along with two white prisoners. The white prisoners had been charged with murder, while Carroll had been convicted for horse theft. The sheriff's newspaper advertisement notes that the prisoners had probably stolen two horses the night they escaped.

Ten months later, on August 30, 1843, the sheriff once again posted a notice for Carroll, who had escaped the county jail the previous day. In this notice, Carroll was described as having an "exceedingly bad look." In the gaps between the 1842 and 1843 notices, we can begin piecing together a story of likely events: Carroll had escaped with the white prisoners, then had been captured and returned. The following summer, he had broken free once again. In these two notices, there is a story of unrelenting commitment to freedom, a politics of obstinacy, and a "bad look"—and several horses stolen.

Reading Carroll's story through these two notices reminds me that escape isn't a onetime thing. Often, it is a series of repeated flights—from the prison, from the plantation, from the strictures of citizenship and nation. I'm thinking about what it takes to run and be captured and decide to run again. I want to believe that Carroll made it across state lines to freedom, that he continued to cow the authorities with his bad look and his hunger for an otherwise. He was in prison for horse stealing, and yet he may have continued to steal horses on his way out—a stubborn disrespect, a raucous refusal.

*   *   *

Throughout the British Caribbean in the seventeenth and eighteenth centuries, it was a common practice for enslaved people to walk behind horses ridden by white riders, often holding the horses' tails to keep up with their pace. In an 1810 book titled *Authentic History of the English West Indies*, the anonymous author writes, "When a West India gentlemen rides out on horseback, he is usually followed by a negro, who runs after him with surprising swiftness." Another observer noted that the footmen would regularly run twelve to fourteen miles behind a horse, "a journey of no considerable exertion for the day."

At the same time, groups of escaped enslaved people in Jamaica established Maroon communities in the mountains of the island. They often raided local plantations, stealing food, tools, and horses. The horses were taught how to navigate the mountainous terrain, how to go where no slave owner could follow. The Maroons were engaged in continuous warfare against plantation owners, and horses were valuable resources to have.

To live like a Maroon, or a fugitive, or a free Black man who escapes prison twice, is to know that theft is a necessary part of liberation. It is to know that you have been lied to about the ways property shapes your existence, and that you have every right to steal your freedom back. When I read the stories of the Taylor brothers or Hardy Carroll or the Maroons who built hidden towns in the crevices of the Blue Mountains, the stories of the many named and unnamed ancestors who brought horses with them on their way to freedom, I want to remember the ways they charted alternate geographies of relation, found co-conspirators where others only saw silent beasts of burden, and made kin amid life-rending brutality.

COWBOY MYTHS

The 2021 Netflix film *The Harder They Fall* is in many ways a classic Western, featuring cowboys, rollicking gunfights, shoot-outs, lovers' arguments in a tavern, a bank holdup, and plenty of swagger. However, it diverges from the classic Western in one important aspect: all of its central characters are Black. Though the story itself is fictionalized, *The Harder They Fall* culls many of its players from the oft-forgotten Black cowboys, cowgirls, and outlaws of the American West, such as Nat Love, Cherokee Bill, and Stagecoach Mary. And the film makes sure viewers are aware of this fact before the story begins, with an emphatic opening text that reads: "While the events of this story are fictional . . . These. People. Existed."

The film centers on cowboy Nat Love, who saw his parents murdered in front of him as a child. After shooting his parents, the killer—an outlaw named Rufus Buck—carves a cross on Love's forehead. Decades later, Nat tracks down

Buck's associate Cortez and kills him in a church. It's only then that Nat realizes his partners, Bill Pickett and Jim Beckwourth, have stolen money that belongs to Buck. He visits his sometime lover Mary Fields (also known as Stagecoach Mary) at the saloon she owns and declares his intentions to seek revenge on Buck.

Meanwhile, Buck's gang, composed of Trudy Smith and Cherokee Bill, is busting him out of prison, killing the soldiers who are keeping him hostage. They make their way to Redwood City, which has served as the center of their operations, and realize it has been under the leadership of a corrupt sheriff. In order to save the town from financial ruin, Buck demands the townspeople raise $50,000.

At Fields's saloon, US Marshal Bass Reeves tells Love that Buck has escaped from prison. Love strikes out on his own to find him, but is soon joined by his friends: Fields, Pickett, Beckwourth, and Cuffee. The gang heads to Redwood in search of Buck and his associates. It is here that the narrative turns itself over to the visual excitement of gunfights and hand-to-hand combat, as the two gangs viciously face off. Love's gang leaves victorious, killing many of Buck's gang members in the process. Away from the maelstrom of the fight, Love and Buck share a quiet moment of reckoning. Buck tells Love that they share a father, and that before Love was born, their father abused and killed Buck's mother. Buck had tracked down Love's family, seeking to avenge his mother's death. Despite this admission, Love kills Buck anyway, finally able to deliver his version of justice.

Love and his friends bury Pickett and Beckwourth, who were both killed in the fight. The cowboys ride off into the proverbial sunset, with Cuffee deciding to join Bass Reeves as a sheriff.

Visually, *The Harder They Fall* is beautiful, with sweeping prairie vistas and stylish fight choreography. The cast boasts big-name Black actors like Idris Elba, Regina King, and LaKeith Stanfield, with Jay-Z and Overbrook Entertainment (a production company cofounded by Will Smith) producing. The film seeks to celebrate the overlooked Black cowboys of the American West, showcasing them in a flashy story of friendship, vengeance, and redemption. Despite reviving an overlooked part of Black history, the film largely follows familiar scripts about the American West. And each time I come across these scripts—uncomplicated images of race and morality, well-established choreographies of outlaw shoot-outs, the erasure of Indigenous communities and narratives—I wonder about the silences that helped create them. I wonder about the stories we could be telling instead: about land theft, about gender and queerness, about Blackness and indigeneity, about love and yearning and desire. About all the forces that came together in shaping this physical and conceptual place we call the "Wild

West" or the "American West." I wonder what fuller, more nuanced tales we could be recuperating from the archive if we weren't concerned with the image of the cowboy on a rearing horse who rides at dawn. I wonder about the violences covered up in service of that myth.

As any reader of fanfiction will know, there's nothing like an unsatisfying narrative to inspire acts of revision and reimagining. While in search of Black histories of the "American West," ones that challenge the glossy, media-friendly stories like *The Harder They Fall*, I also felt drawn to rewrite some of the movie's scenes, to impose my own desires and pleasures onto a story that fell flat for me. It became a way of writing through and with the mythos of the West, of exploring what I (perhaps unfairly) wanted from mainstream cowboy media. Here, you will find some fragments of these fictions, with descriptions of *The Harder They Fall* scenes followed by my italicized retellings.

★　　★　　★

In the corner of a bombed-out house in a shot-up town on the underside of the fight, Trudy Smith and Stagecoach Mary face each other silently, the clicks of their guns cocking, a breathless call and answer. "Trudy's mine," Mary had told Nat Love as the fight picked up. She'd meant it. Mary opens her rifle, letting the bullets fall onto the floor. Trudy lets her bullets fall in one fluid motion, barely moving her hand. "Let's go," Trudy says, her knife against Mary's empty rifle, slashing against Mary's face, whirl of metal against metal against skin. Outside, Nat Love tussles with two men before killing them cleanly. Trudy wrests hold of Mary's rifle and beats her over the head as they fall against the window. They force each other to the ground, Trudy lying in the hay. Trudy reaches for a bottle. The glass breaks.

In the corner of a bombed-out house in a shot-up town on the underside of the fight, Trudy Smith and Stagecoach Mary face each other silently. Mary steadies herself on the sight of Trudy's braids, the march of buttons down the front of Trudy's dress. "Trudy's mine," Mary had told Nat as the fight picked up. She'd meant it. The dust motes floating in the sun make time feel slow-slowslow despite the shouting and running outside. They look shiny in the light, wet somehow, and Mary is reminded of the slickness of Trudy against Mary's empty rifle barrel, of Trudy pushed up against the corner of a horse stall one cold-whipped spring day in Cascade, of Trudy's breaths making little puffs that floated toward Mary as she gently rocked the rifle back and forth, back and forth, as she held Trudy's shuddering shoulders under her free hand. The men outside won't give up for a long time, until many more are dead from stubbornness or pride. The men are focused only on one another now. Mary takes a step forward and holds Trudy's gaze.

I.

I can't remember the first time I heard the song "Home on the Range," but it's been part of my consciousness for most of my life. It's one of the first associations I had with the concept of cowboys, even before I knew much about them beyond outsized, masculine depictions of bluster and bravado. "Home on the Range" was written in the early 1870s by an ear, nose, and throat doctor named Brewster M. Higley. His friend, a violinist named Daniel Kelley, composed music to accompany Higley's lyrics. Higley had traveled from Iowa to settle in Kansas following the Homestead Act of 1862. "Home on the Range" isn't Higley's original title, but an alternate one that became popular as the song took on a life of its own in newspapers and communities throughout the American West.

The song was originally titled with a phrase even more evocative of the desire for ownership, the romantic visions of property, the idea of a divine right to white settlement and expansion that characterized the pioneer era: "My Western Home."

Beginning in the late nineteenth century, millions of settlers journeyed across unknown land to find their western homes. The Homestead Act of 1862 offered 160 acres of land west of the Mississippi to any current or intended citizen of the United States, provided they had never "borne arms" against the US government, and that they live and farm on the land for five years. While the act was seemingly egalitarian—as long as the individual seeking land paid their $18 filing fee and was twenty-one years or older, race and gender was irrelevant—its terms put Black people and Native Americans at a disadvantage. Black people would not become citizens until 1868, and Native Americans would not be granted full citizenship until 1924, making the initial land rush—and ultimately, the allocation of homestead land—dominated by white settlers. By 1986, when the last federal homesteading program ended in Alaska, 270 million acres of former Indian Territory had been given away.

Among the white settlers who traveled west in search of land was the Wilder family, whose journeys are chronicled in the *Little House on the Prairie* books, written by Laura Ingalls Wilder. The series follows Wilder's pioneer family as they move through what we now call the Midwest and finally to a homestead in South Dakota. In their first homesteading venture, the Ingalls move to Kansas, lured by dreams of uncrowded landscapes, new opportunity, and charismatic megafauna. Laura's pa is the architect of these visions, convincing the family to move to a place where "the wild animals lived without being afraid . . . the little fawns and their mothers . . . the fat, lazy bears." Pa wants to move to the West where the land stretches out in large expanses, "and there were no settlers. Only Indians lived there."

*   *   *

Cherokee Bill, Angel, and Trudy have found their way to the back of the train car, past the wall of white soldiers, the shocked and terrified white train passengers. They are here to free their imprisoned friend, Rufus Buck. Cherokee Bill has counted down and threatened an "officiant of the goddamn law." He has lieutenant-marched the young son of one of the soldiers into this last car. Cherokee Bill and Angel and Trudy reach a large blue metal door. Trudy lays one gloved hand against it, caressing it almost, placing an ear to it. She turns to one of the soldiers. "Open it," she says. She needs to show him a government document first, of course, needs to scare him into submission with the threat of his corruption being exposed. When Rufus Buck finally emerges from the train car, he shares a long look with Trudy, then lays his head on her shoulder. He touches his forehead to Cherokee Bill's forehead. He takes a long, deep breath before the officiants of the goddamn law unlock his chains.

In my version of this story, the embraces between Rufus and Nat, and Rufus and Trudy would last forever. The world would halt for the hundreds of words held in the glances between friends and comrades, for the first moments of a man released from imprisonment. In my version of this story, a thousand chains would fall throughout the wild, wild West as the chains were unlocked from a captive man's ankles. In my version of this story, there is time enough and time enough and infinite time for the first embrace after prison, for the love and sorrow shared between a Black man and the friends who shot through a train of white passengers and officiants of the goddamn law to get him free.

II.

There is no mention of Indigenous people in *The Harder They Fall*, although the lives of Black and Indigenous communities were deeply intertwined in the western territories. Two characters in the film, Rufus Buck and Cherokee Bill, had Indigenous ancestry in real life. Buck's gang was composed of Creek brothers Sam Sampson and Maoma July, Black Creek freedmen Lewis and Lucky Davis, and himself. In the summer of 1895, the Buck gang wrought terror in Oklahoma territory. They robbed a general store and murdered several people, including Deputy Marshal John Garrett. In the only existing image of the gang, they stand shoulder to shoulder, arms touching. All wear cowboy hats cocked at various angles and stare directly into the camera. Buck stands in the middle wearing a dark overcoat. His face is the most gaunt, his eyes the most fixed, the whites of his pupils starkly visible even in the gentle sepia-toned blur of the photo. He was twenty-one when he was hanged.

This story is somehow even more gruesome than that of the film's Rufus Buck, and that discrepancy feels important to know. Rather than the endless 2D prairies and glamorous montage shots, I'm more interested in the bloody and unresolved histories of the Black people who struggled and fought and shaped lives in the West, who committed acts of irredeemable violence and unimaginable care. Part of the cultural project of films like *The Harder They Fall* is a project of respectability. While there is violence portrayed in the film, and an excess of bad intent, the characters' motivations are flattened into caricatures, never connected to larger issues of land dispossession or post-Reconstruction racial politics. The simplistic message never travels far from the surface: Black people were cowboys too. The film's analysis of history seems to stop there, preventing it from fully exploring the crucial, glorious messiness of the Black archive.

*   *   *

The Crimson Hood gang is galloping through the mountains, whooping and hollering as they go. On their heads: faded pink masks showing only their eyes and mouths. In their saddlebags: a collective $25,000 in cash. There's nothing like a successful bank robbery to raise one's spirits. They don't know it yet, but they are racing toward the end of their lives. Half a mile away, sharpshooter Bill Pickett is waiting behind the rocks, rifle at the ready. Pickett flips his lucky coin, then readies his weapon. Soon, Crimson Hoods and their horses are falling to the ground in all directions.

Okay, so you see them galloping and you see them falling to the ground and it would be reasonable to assume they're dead. But what you don't know is that every Crimson Hood member, every single one, has a mojo bag tucked between his saddle and his horse. A little leather number filled with stones and herbs they cannot name, a guarantee of protection. The mojo bags came from Bose James, who got them from his momma, who carried her spirits, her plants, her prayers with her when she was brought from Mississippi to Brazos County, Texas, in 1857. She spent her life training horses on the plantation, broke each arm in multiple places, was in the saddle nearly till the day she died. When Bose said he was leaving for Oklahoma to try his luck, she told him to wait till the moon was right. She gave him these bags, told him to share with the men he'd ride with—he would know what she meant soon enough. When Pickett's bullets hit the Crimson Hoods' bodies, they turned and rode in the other direction, obscured by a haze of dust. I can't speak for the bodies lying on the ground, but I saw each of those Crimson Hoods alive and well at a tavern in Oklahoma City last night. Don't trust everything you think you see.

III.

Running for eight years, from 1949 to 1957, the television show *The Lone Ranger* featured a white Texas Ranger and his Indigenous sidekick Tonto. In the show's premiere episode, Tonto saves the Lone Ranger's life after he has been attacked by outlaws. Nobly self-sacrificing, Tonto is portrayed as a subservient and loyal supporting character to the Lone Ranger's dashing figure. Tonto was played by Jay Silverheels, a Canadian Mohawk actor originally from the Six Nations Reserve. Silverheels was "discovered while touring with his indoor lacrosse team, and soon began a career in acting." In 1969, while appearing on *The Tonight Show*, Silverheels did a satirical take on his long-standing role as Tonto. He adopted the pidgin spoken by his former character and explained that he was an unemployed worker whose résumé included "working thirty years as a faithful sidekick . . . thirty lousy years."

The Lone Ranger was modeled after the real Texas Rangers, a militia considered the first state law enforcement body in the United States. The Texas Rangers were founded by Stephen Austin, a land contractor intent on bringing the

Mexican territory under US rule. Austin started this project by bringing three hundred white settler families and their slaves to Texas in 1825. He fought for slavery to be introduced into Texas and advocated for the extermination of the Indigenous Karankawa people of the region. In an 1836 speech in defense of Texan independence from the Mexican government, Austin argued that "a few years back Texas was a wilderness, the home of the uncivilized and wandering Comanche and other tribes of Indians. . . . In order to restrain these savages and bring them into subjection, the government opened Texas for settlement."

Austin created the Texas Rangers in 1823 to protect those living in his colony of settlers. Feeling the Mexican government's militias were insufficient, he hired a group of ten men to patrol the colony and surrounding areas for "errant thieves united with Indians." The Texas Rangers continued to operate even after the Texas Revolution, contributing to conflicts with Indigenous people whose land was being settled by white families. They also took part in the Mexican-American War and gained notoriety for their military skills. In 1858, a group of rangers murdered eight hundred Indigenous people in an apparent attempt to enact revenge for a raid. The rangers also became known for their significant role in La Matanza and Hora de Sangre (1910–20), a period of concerted violence defined by regular murders and disappearances of Tejanos and Mexicanos.

In its ongoing attempt to fully control Texas territory and make it a white settlement, absent of the Indigenous people who made it a "wilderness," the US government enlisted the help of the Indigenous Seminole from Florida. The logics of colonial expansion sometimes appear to contradict themselves, complicated by the creation of acceptable minorities and the exploitation of existing community divisions. But the central, driving force behind the act remains the same: to extract as much as possible from the people and the land. To enlist any available life into the project of the nation, its self-serving myths, its relentless economies of violence.

Among the Seminoles who migrated to Texas and worked for the government during this time was a Black Seminole woman named Johanna July. July's family signed a contract with the army in 1871, and she grew up breaking horses at the Fort Clark army post. In the Works Progress Administration interview conducted with July, she talked about training horses from a young age and being exempt from regular women's tasks because of her skill in riding. Editorializing freely, the transcriber wrote that July "lived the life of a carefree Indian boy."

July's riding skills served her well as an adult when she escaped on horseback from an abusive marriage. Riding forty-five miles in one night, she made it to safety on the back of an old pony who wouldn't go faster than a trot.

Her ex-husband came after her several times, unsuccessfully shooting at her and trying to lasso her with a rope. She eluded him every time. "I got to the brush an' he never could find me," July said in the interview. "He would have killed me, an' I knowed it!"

IV.

In *The Harder They Fall*, the character Cuffee is based on Cathay Williams. Williams served in the Civil War under the name William Cathay and worked for the army in a capacity only men were permitted to. Williams was honorably discharged in 1868 after an army surgeon reported the soldier was a woman. Throughout the film, Cuffee dresses identically to the other men, until Nat Love needs someone to rob a bank with him. He calls Cuffee to him and throws a package onto the ground. It contains a red dress, and the surrounding men laugh. The whole situation is framed as comedic. After an initial refusal, Cuffee undresses in the midst of the others, and Jim jokes that he thought he'd fallen for a man. Struggling with the difficulties of riding in a skirt, Cuffee awkwardly accompanies Nat to hold up a bank at gunpoint. In the process, a further disrobing: Nat asks for Cuffee's legal name.

In an interview, Danielle Deadwyler—the actress who

plays Cuffee—also described the scene as a funny one. "That's the beauty of comedy, right?" Danielle said. "It's like, oh, she's defined herself as this hard-ass ball buster . . . and then, the one thing she has to do is put on a dress." When I watched this scene, it seemed like the filmmakers had decided Cuffee needed to be humbled somehow; the character's gender nonconformity was too threatening to exist on-screen without being made into a joke. In the same interview, Deadwyler went on to say the "contrast" between the dress and Cuffee's normal clothes is part of what creates the comedy. Yet somehow, when Cuffee is forced to strip down in front of a group of men, it doesn't seem funny.

V.

In October 2022, I attended an experimental theater piece called *high noon* at Philadelphia's FringeArts festival. The piece was created by a group of Black queer and trans artists who were exploring the figure of the cowboy and what it might mean to them. At the beginning of the piece, a single figure sat alone on the stage: a Black person wearing a brown cowboy hat, a brown leather harness over a white T-shirt, and dark pants, staring silently at the floor. *high noon* had a pervasive sense of loneliness that struck me as different from the traditional portrayals of the solitary cowboy on the range or the pioneer families settling into new territory. For most of the show, only one or two actors were onstage at the same time. When the actors sang or spoke about being alone, or being alone while feeling constantly surveilled, or about the contradictions and impossibilities of freedom, they weren't just describing a situational experience. They were speaking to fundamental truths about what it is to be a Black person in a country built on Manifest Destiny, living in the ever-present shadows of the "Wild West," haunted by its foundational myths of white nationhood and conquest.

I felt that haunting when I watched the scenes with Cuffee and the red dress. Living in the Wild West offers some opportunities for expansive self-expression, yet Cuffee is still ultimately policed and surveilled, forced to step into a dress in service of a "larger cause." In the process of undressing, Cuffee's genitals become the center of Jim's joke about a queer desire that almost reads as a thwarted disruption of the status quo. Having watched *high noon*, I want more for Cuffee. I want them to drape themselves in the longing and desire that winds like a whisper through *The Harder They Fall*, to find in their loneliness others like themselves. I want them to clothe themselves in denim and leather without the specter of the red dress. I want for them the space to name themselves without the violence of a forced unbecoming. This feeling is familiar to me—meeting a Black, queer character who gestures to impossible worlds, worlds unable to exist within the universe of the work.

high noon was the first place I saw Black queer and trans people take on the image of the cowboy and speak to it in a way that felt irreverent, experimental, true to the seductiveness and complexity of the figure and what it stands for. Like so much of mainstream media about cowboys, *The Harder They Fall* relegates queer histories to the realm of subtext and implication. In *high noon*, I learned something about the love it takes to dismantle a colonial myth and look for the possibilities of what it has foreclosed: vulnerability, anger, queer heartache, despair. In *high noon*'s interpretation, the cowboy is not a figure of victory and indestructability, but a tragic symbol of the devastation caused by colonial expansion and the lies of American exceptionalism.

Those of us whose histories have been obscured, excluded, or mistold by colonial archives are often tasked with filling in narrative gaps. As I engaged with mythical representations of the cowboy, I turned to the counterarchive for truer depictions of the people who had made lives in the American West. This counterarchive, this shadow history, was one I found in many places: books by authors who researched the history of queer and African American rodeo circuits; personal accounts of people who settled the West, or whose land was settled as it became known as the West, or who provided forced labor for the settler project; oral histories that were held in government archives but nonetheless gestured toward truths that challenged the authoritative narrative. But even with these sources, I was aware there were countless stories I could never know. Some of those stories would have been withheld for fear of censorship or criminalization, and some would have been purposely suppressed by history's official stenographers. I feel deep respect for those with the skills and foresight to dodge the questioning gaze of the archives. At the same time, while reckoning with these silences and unknowns, I turned to the practice of speculation, or what some might call informed conjecture. For scholar Saidiya Hartman, "critical fabulation" is the use of storytelling and imaginative practices as a way of relating to archival absence. In Hartman's *Wayward Lives, Beautiful Experiments: Intimate Histories of Riotous Black Girls, Troublesome Women, and Queer Radicals*, she writes about young Black women in Philadelphia and New York who troubled the boundaries of gender and family with their radical approaches to labor, sex, and intimate relations. Drawing on an array of sources including state archives and photographs, she imagines the ways they flirted with their lovers, organized in their communities, and adorned themselves beyond the watchful eyes of journalists and social workers. In a similar way, *high noon* provided me with a model of relating to the cowboy myth in a way that was both speculative and archivally grounded. *high noon* showed me what it might be like, even in the midst of careful research, to create my own expanses, my own alluring and mythic figures, to people a page or a show with Black queer folks insistent on the power of their own bodily archives.

I found myself most touched by the monologues in *high noon*, the lyrical and meandering meditations delivered by Black folks wrestling with the cowboy, the violence and promise of concepts like *wilderness* and *expanse*. Behind them, images were projected onto a large screen: the composer Coleridge-Taylor Perkinson, desert scenery, groups of horses. One actor delivered lines I still think about almost every day: "There are two freedoms. One that compels you to chase and race me, and one that is why I will never get ahead. I will always choose the second."

VI.

At the end of *Little House on the Prairie*, Laura and her family are forced to leave their homestead because the government has ordered white settlers out of that section of Indian Territory. As they prepare to leave in their covered wagon, Pa takes out his fiddle and starts singing:

And we'll rally round the flag, boys,
We'll rally once again,
Shouting the battle-cry of Freedom!

So often the "freedoms" Black people are granted—those we are told we should be grateful for—are elaborate excuses for new reasons to be surveilled and oppressed, new ways to be chased and raced by those intent on our destruction. So often the personal liberties of people like Pa are built on the absence of our own. What we know as the Wild West would not exist without the 182,000 enslaved people living in Texas in 1860, brought to the Mexican territory by white cattle ranchers, farmers, and speculators pursuing their dreams of wealth and westward expansion. It would not exist without the knowledge of horseback riding and cattle herding these Black people carried with them, the former enslaved people who became hired cowhands after emancipation.

In her poem "Out West," Donika Kelly writes, "Refuse the old means of measurement. / Rely instead on the thrumming / wilderness of self. . . . Do not wander. We are all apportioned / a certain measure of stillness." Maybe Black folks never went looking for the cowboy as much as we were searching for a place to be. A stolen people on the run, a whispered dream of freedom. A fictional expanse inviting us into a vast and uninterrupted wilderness of the self.

DANCEHALL RODEO

Igrew up far from the states considered part of the Wild West, far from the contested borderlands now understood as Texas, and unlike Nat Love or Stagecoach Mary or Pa or Tonto, I have never been west of the Mississippi. As the child of immigrants from Jamaica and the Philippines, I can't claim the American West or its inhabitants as a part of my ancestral lineage. But my people, too, have been shaped by the imaginary of the Wild West and its exports. The cultural context that created the Lone Ranger and Tonto, the swaggering movie cowboys played by actors like Clint Eastwood and John Wayne, the popularity of *Little House on the Prairie*, and even the revisionist projects of *The Harder They Fall* and *high noon* has never been confined to the United States.

In 1982, over thirty years after the first *Lone Ranger* episode aired on television, a Jamaican dancehall artist named Lone Ranger made an album titled *Hi-Yo, Silver, Away!* In the album, he sings about marijuana ("Legalize the National Herb"), unfaithful women ("Love Affair Problem"), and class issues ("Living as a Poor"). As in many dancehall albums of the era, *Hi-Yo, Silver, Away!* is suffused with gunslinging braggadocio. In the song "Lone Ranger and Tonto," Lone Ranger sings about a figure who walks into the bar to start a "likkle war," bearing "the taste of liquor and the smell of cigar." On the album cover, the title is written in a lasso-inspired font. The cover displays a series of comic book panels, forming an illustrated story about cowboys fighting at a saloon. In one of the panels, a group of cowboys sits at a domino table, yelling at one another. The conflict escalates, with one man getting pounded over the head with a chair. The comic ends with the saloon trashed, two cowboys riding away, and a figure silhouetted against the moon saying "Hi-Yo, Silver, Away!"

Jamaica in the early 1980s was marked by violent political divisions, unemployment, and poverty caused by the continued influence of colonial powers. After gaining independence from England in 1962, Jamaica struggled to be economically self-sufficient. American and Canadian corporations ravaged the countryside with open-pit bauxite mining, occupying agricultural lands and contributing to widespread displacement. Jamaica was forced to borrow money from the International Monetary Fund, and the predatory terms and austerity measures accompanying these loans further destabilized the economy. In 1980, Edward Seaga, representing the Jamaica Labour Party, won the presidential election over the democratic socialist People's National Party candidate, Michael Manley. Under Seaga's leadership, Jamaica solidified its relationship with the International Monetary Fund, coming away with over 4.6 billion dollars in debt.

During this period, dancehall was rapidly growing as a popular cultural form. Emerging from the more traditionally moral and laid-back sounds of roots reggae, dancehall was, as its name suggests, centered in the collective and youthful exuberance of Kingston party spaces. Energized by new audio technologies that allowed sampling and computerized production, dancehall reflected the anxieties, preoccupations, and aesthetics of a younger generation. This generation—the rudeboys and posses, the DJs and producers who defined '80s and '90s dancehall—created music that was irrevocably shaped by the economic precarity of the era.* Both urban and rural workers were leaving Jamaica in large numbers due to a lack of job opportunities. There was a shortage of musicians who could perform live, leading DJs to focus on developing ways of listening to recorded music. Most of their efforts focused on sound systems: large sets of

---

* While I don't get into it here, the rise of dancehall also saw the increasing presence of women in popular Jamaican music. This was the era of the "dancehall queen," represented by iconic artists like Lady Saw, Sister Nancy, and Lady G. While these women artists didn't engage as much with the imagery of the cowboy, their work reflected the diasporic cross-pollination, turbulent political climate, and technological innovations that characterized dancehall music during the 1980s and 1990s.

speakers and amplifiers designed to blast music outdoors. These mobile installations could be wheeled around, re-configured, set up on a street corner or in the middle of an empty lot. At a time when many people could not afford to buy records, and Jamaican radio stations weren't playing the reggae and American music people wanted to hear, sound systems facilitated collective listening experiences. They also functioned as forums for news and political analysis, with mic'd-up DJs providing commentary over the music.

Jamaican sound system innovations became essential to artists who were shaping the roots of hip-hop in American cities. As Jeff Chang writes in *Can't Stop Won't Stop: A History of the Hip-Hop Generation*, "The blues had Mississippi, jazz had New Orleans. Hip-hop has Jamaica." In the South Bronx, Jamaican-born artist DJ Kool Herc was helping to spearhead the development of hip-hop. Black American rappers like Run-D.M.C. were releasing collaborations with dancehall artists like Yellowman. And hip-hop artists were incorporating the riffing and rhyming practices of dancehall MCs into the evolving genre of rap.

It was within this context that Jamaican artists began using the imagery of American cowboy films. Beginning in the early twentieth century, movie theaters were an increasingly significant part of Jamaican leisure life. The Carib Theatre in Kingston, which opened in 1938, was once the highest-grossing cinema in the Caribbean. By the 1980s, even smaller rural parishes often had at least one cinema. Cinemas also doubled as performance halls, hosting everything from talent shows to internationally known celebrities. These performance halls provided chances for local musicians to be "discovered" and were known as places where one's dreams of entertainment industry fame could become reality. From its advent, the movie theater industry in Jamaica was intertwined with American capital. The Carib Theatre was built after Jamaican businessman B. M. Andrade partnered with the American film production and distribution company Metro-Goldwyn-Mayer (MGM). Seeing opportunity in the Jamaican market, MGM constructed the Carib Theatre to compete with Jamaican-owned cinemas like those of Audrey Morais. This American influence also shaped the kinds of media that were available to Jamaican audiences; for example, the Carib Theatre was able to secure exclusive rights to MGM and 20th Century Fox films. As American corporations continued to push cultural exports in Jamaica, local audiences were introduced to Wild West characters like the Lone Ranger and Josey Wales.

There were artists who produced music under names like Clint Eastwood, Lee Van Cleef, and John Wayne, all homages to the men whose faces had become synonymous with the filmic American West. Other artists took on names modeled after real or fictional cowboys themselves, such as Josey Wales and Johnny Ringo. And like

Lone Ranger and the album *Hi-Yo, Silver, Away!*, many of these artists incorporated language and images from Hollywood's Wild West into their work. Beginning in the 1970s, producer and singer Lee "Scratch" Perry released several records referencing cowboy Westerns, including *Clint Eastwood* and *Eastwood Rides Again*. The word "posse," which came to signify Jamaican gangs, was also drawn from Westerns, where a posse was a group of cowboys who helped a sheriff fight crime.

The early years of dancehall saw the emergence of "slackness": a culture of sexually explicit lyrics that exchanged the suggestiveness of older genres for graphic descriptions that left nothing to the imagination. Dancehall songs often focused on stories of love, fights, and sexual conquest. However, the genre also engaged deeply with the political moment. In songs like Yellowman's "Soldier Take Over" and "Operation Eradication," artists talked about experiences of growing up in poverty and decried the partisan violence that filled Kingston's streets. While Jamaican artists took on the names and mythologies of filmic cowboys, their interpretations diverged in many ways from the histories of the American West.

These uniquely Jamaican versions of the cowboy myth were shaped by many realities, including the island's position as a majority-Black country and former sugarcane economy (in contrast to the American context of settler colonialism and westward expansion). However, one key factor in Jamaican cowboy narratives was the criminalization of dancehall culture itself. Dancehall was firmly a genre of the proletariat, arising from the everyday struggles and concerns of poor people on the island. Wealthier Jamaicans saw dancehall culture as lewd and disruptive, a haven for gang violence and social unrest. Dancehalls—the general term for indoor and outdoor sites where people gathered to play this music—were regularly raided by police under the guise of public safety. As Norman C. Stolzoff writes in *Wake the Town and Tell the People: Dancehall Culture in Jamaica*, "The police see dancehalls not only as giving refuge to gangsters, but as places where victories over the police are celebrated." As places where poor people could congregate, gain political consciousness, and engage in social critique, dancehalls posed a threat to colonial Jamaican society. They were also spaces where underground economies flourished. The characters of the Wild West cowboy and outlaw became a way for artists to tell stories about class disparity, interactions with policing, and literal examples of running from the law. In their music, dancehall artists took creative liberties with the moral universe of the Hollywood Western. In cowboy movies, a posse was on the side of the law, helping to catch the bad guys. But on the streets of Kingston, the posses were those oppressed and targeted by respectable society, the "ghetto youths" fighting back against the police.

Album cover for Lone Ranger's *Hi-Yo, Silver, Away!*

The figure of the Wild West cowboy is a slippery one, changing form through space and time, offering up a fantasy of dangerousness and self-possession that is both distinct and endlessly adaptable. For early Jamaican dancehall artists and the generations that grew up on their music, the cowboy Western became a language for rhyming about colonial dispossession and righteous rebellion, on sound system rhythms that were larger than life.

PONY BOOKS

Around the age of six or seven, I received a boxed set of pony books as a gift. The set contained the books *Black Beauty*, *My Friend Flicka*, and *National Velvet* as well as a horse pendant that hung from a delicate silver chain. After reading these books, I began to pay attention to the kids riding horses near the baseball field in Prospect Park. Soon after, I started to ask for riding lessons. In this way, my origin story as a rider and horse lover is inextricable from my life as a reader.

I use the phrase "pony books" here to refer to a genre of children's literature centered on horses and the kids who love and ride them. Ironically, Anna Sewell's *Black Beauty*, considered one of the significant predecessors to twentieth-century pony books, is not about children at all. It focuses instead on the cruel treatment of horses, providing a treatise on the way laboring animals were abused in the late nineteenth century. Until World War II, the pony book genre was centered in England, with many books featuring working animals or technical advice on horse care. During this time period, the genre was largely geared toward boys; riding and working with horses was mainly a men's activity. After the war, as an increasingly prosperous middle class created a consumer base for leisure activities, more pony books featured girls who rode and owned horses for fun. British authors like the Pullein-Thompson sisters, K. M. Peyton, and Ruby Ferguson wrote girl characters navigating family life, friendship, and the world of competitive riding. In the United States, some postwar pony media engaged with the mythology of the American West, such as the 1946 film adaptation of Will James's *Smoky*, about the adventures of a cowboy and his horse. Others, similarly to their British counterparts, featured children's adventures with their ponies at boarding stables and in idyllic landscapes. As the twentieth century progressed, American children's literature became dominated by series fiction. In the 1990s and early 2000s, several influential pony book series began to be published, including Bonnie Bryant's the Saddle Club, Joanna Campbell's Thoroughbreds, and Lauren Brooke's Chestnut Hill.

It was here, in the pages of pony books, that I learned some of my earliest literary lessons about class, gender, and what it meant to be a child who loved horses. In contrast to stereotypes of the horse world as being one of extreme elitism and wealth, the protagonists in these books are often presented as respectably middle class. They're portrayed as girls next door who have to grind for what they have. The protagonist of *National Velvet* is a butcher's daughter who starts the book riding paper cutout horses from magazines. She inherits a horse from one of her father's customers and becomes a champion racer. When Velvet wins the Grand National race, she refuses offers of publicity and media coverage, insisting that her horse was the true winner. In the Chestnut Hill books, practical, kind scholarship student Malory is the child of a small-town shoe store owner. She finds it hard to fit in with the other girls at her monied boarding school but shines when she's riding and training horses. Of course, because these characters' class backgrounds are mostly described in comparison to their one-percenter peers, we get a skewed view of their circumstances. Most of their families own horses and suburban homes; they're hardly struggling financially. But the books make a virtue out of the idea (or illusion) of humble beginnings, contrasting unpretentious, hardworking heroines with their gauche, arrogant rich-girl enemies. In the first book of the Saddle Club series, new rider Lisa starts a friendship with Veronica, the stable's resident mean girl. When she visits Veronica's house, Lisa is shocked at the grandeur she sees. Lisa "had lived all her life in nice middle-class neighborhoods and nice middle-class homes," but "Veronica had apparently spent her life living in a palace." Lisa realizes the reason Veronica is so good at ordering people around at the stable is because she honed those skills at home, with a maid, gardener, and chauffeur at her service.

In keeping with an age-old formula, the callow, arrogant rich girls always get their comeuppance in the end. The entitlement they cultivate as a result of their money and power is often their downfall, leading them to be uncaring friends, reckless students, and irresponsible horse owners. Pony books emphasized the importance of good character, but they also inculcated me in the myth of meritocracy. In Lisa and Veronica and Malory's world, wealthy people's money can buy them fancy horses, nice clothes, and palatial homes. However, these affordances are never portrayed as significant or even that useful. Being industrious and thrifty will always bring the biggest rewards. It's a narrative formula that teaches readers they can always outwork a rich, mean girl, material advantages be damned. While the optimism is admirable, these stories also encourage wishful thinking about the actual effects of economic disparities, a belief that personal goodness can solve injustices that have been centuries in the making.

Other than pony books, my favorite book series in elementary school were historical: the American Girl, Royal

Diaries, and Dear America books, which dramatized past events through the lens of children's everyday lives. I consumed classic turn-of-the-century novels about spunky white girls by authors like L. M. Montgomery. I read fantasy series like *Eragon* and *Redwall*. And I loved the work of Virginia Hamilton, who, in addition to writing the seminal *The People Could Fly: American Black Folktales*, also wrote chapter books like *M. C. Higgins, the Great*. Looking back, I would say that my reading life made me feel empowered. The books I read encouraged me to explore the imaginative possibilities of my world, to engage with history from a position of curiosity, to take risks, and to believe that the mundanities of my life were a story worth telling. When I think about pony books now, I'm grateful for the ways they emboldened me to believe that being a rider was something within reach for me too. If I had read books in which the Veronicas of the world ruled the stables and everyone else resentfully accepted that, I don't know if I would have asked my parents for riding lessons. Still, I wonder what a different pony book genre would look like, one that gave kids a way to think about class and inequality that was neither fatalistic nor naive. So often, the popular narrative forms of children's literature mirror dominant cultural narratives about individual achievement and fortitude in the face of adversity. But what if the rich girl's oppressiveness wasn't just written as a behavior issue? What if the shocking wealth of

Veronica's family didn't go unquestioned—what if we were told something about its origins? What if our determined heroines knew that they shouldn't have to meet each day with resourcefulness and good cheer while compensating for the massive inequalities that shaped their world?

I admit that I might sound didactic—after all, pony books aren't meant to be political treatises. However, seeing children's literature as fluffy or "just for fun" risks overlooking the significant ways that it both reflects and co-creates a collective political consciousness. As evidenced by conservative book bans and recent proposals to scrub histories of slavery and colonialism from school curricula, determining what children read has become a site of intense contestation. The books children read are a marker of the values held by the adults around them, and the kinds of futures those adults believe in. In *Learning from the Left: Children's Literature, the Cold War, and Radical Politics in the United States*, Julia L. Mickenberg traces a history of leftist children's literature throughout the twentieth century. Mickenberg finds that children's literature often went overlooked by those wanting to censor leftist media, even during the McCarthy era. This created space for authors, artists, librarians, publishers, and booksellers to distribute literature that did many of the things mainstream pony books (and children's literature as a whole) did not: challenge ideals of individualism and meritocracy, illuminate class structures, and encourage readers to question US militarism and propaganda. The books Mickenberg discusses show that it's possible to have a children's literature that is both playful and critical, attentive to the larger structures that impact our lives while still rich with character development and agency. Regardless of what they are, the ideologies contained within works of children's literature don't happen accidentally. While pony books might seem like relatively low-stakes and leisurely reads, they are also works that reflect specific political conditions—the consolidation of the children's publishing industry, the surveillance of leftist movements, and prevailing stories about labor, money, and power that continue to shape new generations of readers.

★   ★   ★

Many pony book heroines have a special bond with horses who are too difficult or traumatized for others to work with. Often, the heroine herself has gone through hardship that enables her to empathize with the horse. In the Heartland series, Amy loses her mom to a horrific accident before becoming a successful trainer who rehabilitates formerly abused horses. Both Carole in the Saddle Club series and Malory in the Chestnut Hill series have deceased parents. Multiple characters in the Thoroughbred series experience loss and family trauma, which sometimes threatens to end their riding careers.

While the concept of protagonists triumphing over hardships is a common one, pony books were one of the first places where I saw trauma and struggle framed as strengths. It wasn't just that the characters had gone through loss or bullying, or that their families couldn't afford horses. It was that they were somehow better for having gone through these things, endowed with a tenacity and emotional capacity that enriched them as riders and horse trainers. This is a specific kind of capitalist morality tale—personal hardship builds character, and if your pain can make you better at your job, you're all the better for it. At the same time, seeing trauma and hurt as a site of connection shaped the way I viewed the world. Until I began reading pony books in earnest, I had been used to seeing pain and sadness as things that alienated you from others, creating a gulf that could never be bridged with words. Being schooled at home meant I had no classmates to commiserate with, and it sometimes felt like I was speaking a different emotional language than the other kids I met. They could never know what it was like. But in pony books, being traumatized or lonely also meant you had access to more capacious ways of communicating with others, more skills for reaching outside yourself and building intimacy with another living being. This is an idealized vision, which also fails to account for the lasting and debilitating effects of trauma. But in some ways, I later found parts of that vision to be true. As I got older, I found others who knew what it was like to grow up emotionally isolated, to be coerced into emotional caretaking for a parent, to be an oldest sibling in a volatile family setting. I found that the experiences that made me feel most alone could also be shared languages, portals into more deeply knowing another, invitations to ask more of the world. While I never had my dramatic moment with a troublesome rescue horse, I learned that the skills of vigilant observation and emotional sensitivity I had been forced to cultivate served me well as a rider, helping me to notice horses' personalities and cues, clueing me in to the stories that lived in the body yet went unspoken.

With some exceptions, pony books are a genre created about and for girls. Pony books contain a veritable catalog of girlhood archetypes, from defiant tomboy to sensitive, intuitive animal lover to prissy, hyperfeminine diva. As an older teen, I realized that "girl" was an inaccurate identifier for me, mostly an ill-fitting expectation assigned to me by other people. But when I was a young reader who hadn't yet come into language for a trans identity, pony books offered an expansive set of possibilities for the kinds of girls I might embody. I identified with many of these archetypes at various times, trying them on for size as I played pretend or ran around with kids in the neighborhood. Pony books helped me figure out what I did want from my girlhood: the models of passionate and committed friendship, the many stories about girls who understood and took care of animals, the rakish dirtbag vibes of characters who were covered in horsehair most of the time. The category of "horse girl," as distinct from simply "girl," held possibilities of mischief and self-expression that called out to me from the pages of the books I read. Throughout the course of writing this book, I reread many of the pony books that at one time filled my childhood bookshelves. I downloaded most of them from the internet, highlighting quotes on my tablet to return to later. My collection of pony books still exists in physical form, but they are packed away in boxes in my family apartment. When I became estranged from a family member in 2023, I relinquished my already tenuous access to many things that were mine, including artifacts of my (horse) girlhood. I can't get those copies now, and so I find other ways to reach them, typing remembered titles into search boxes and following nested trails of hyperlinks. In the same way that pony books gave me access to a chimeric sense of girlhood that was never really mine, I still turn to them now to help me access something I can't touch with my hands.

In the essay "Arriving at Desire," Trinidadian writer Dionne Brand describes her childhood reading of the salacious classic of British literature *Lady Chatterley's Lover*. In high school, Brand and her peers passed around a copy of the book, hiding it in a brown paper wrapping. She writes:

> *I do not know among us who identified with the lady and who with the gamekeeper. The book's gendering could not have been seamless. No book's gendering can be, ultimately, since a book asks us to embody, which at once takes us across borders of all kinds. . . . Anyway, some of us were him and some of us were her. . . . Both the possibilities and constraints of enactment existed within the borderless territory of the book.*

Brand goes on to discuss the simultaneous familiarity and alienation she and her classmates felt when reading about the character of Lady Chatterley. While the wealthy baronet's wife shared little with the girls attending school on a Caribbean island, the themes of the book beckoned them into a readerly place of slippage and transformation. "The conversation going on in the book was one about culture, class, technology, and sexuality," Brand writes. "It was the same conversation going on in our lives." Brand and her classmates also felt an internal tension, a "cleavage" between the world of the book and the place where they lived, "on an island at the bottom of the New World." In Brand's recollection, I recognize the ways that pony books also beckoned me across borders, inviting me to understand my own embodied experience through encounters with characters whose lives and racialized genderings were very different from my own. When I was a young reader, pony books beckoned me and said, *Here is how to be a girl; here is how to be good. Here is what you must do about the things you do not have. Here is an open expanse—trouble it as you will.*

NOTHING WITHOUT EACH OTHER

I n middle and high school, *The Saddle Club*'s Carole Hanson was the girl I thought I could be. Based on the book series written by Bonnie Bryant, the television series followed Carole and her two best friends, Lisa and Stevie, as they navigated life as burgeoning equestrians (and adolescents) at the fictional Pine Hollow Stables. In between grooming ponies, going on trail rides, and getting lessons from resident horse trainer Max, the friends solved mysteries and fought off rich mean girls Veronica and Christy. Carole—played by the actress Keenan MacWilliam—was in school, but the pressures of homework or academic achievement never seemed to play a part in her life. She wasn't rich like Veronica and Christy, but money was never a worry, seeing as she was able to afford having a horse. And while her mom was dead, she had her dad and a loving circle of friends and mentors.

Carole had what I thought at the time was a great sense of style. She wore stretchy riding pants in cool colors (purple!), quilted vests, and cozy sweaters for when the autumn breeze blew through Pine Hollow. And she wanted to be a veterinarian, just like me. Whenever Carole appeared on my television, I felt a thrill of recognition and desire. Because she existed, a part of me could exist too. It was a part of me that was already being lost to the demands of older siblinghood, academic achievement, and a carefully curated facade of skepticism: the part of me that loved ponies with a wide-eyed awe, that was enchanted by a life where grief and loneliness seemed surmountable, the part of me that wanted to live in a magical middle-of-nowhere town where the hottest after-school hangout was the stable. Every time I watched *The Saddle Club* and listened to the theme song "Hello World" by Belle Perez ("Hello world, this is me / Life should be fun for everyone"), just for a moment, I could let myself believe it was really that simple.

In addition to being fashionable and having a pony, Carole was the only Black character on the show for the first two seasons—which were the only seasons that I watched (the third and final season was released in 2008, five years after the end of season two). Carole was also the only canonically Black rider in the book series. The two other members of the Saddle Club, Stevie and Lisa, were both white, and so were the other kids and adults who surrounded Carole at Pine Hollow. In the world of *The Saddle Club*, race is never acknowledged. As is typical of TV's token Black girls, the actor who played Carole was light-skinned, with hazel eyes and dark brown curls. In the books, she is described only as "African American," and Carole's skin tone varies from book cover to book cover. But on TV, Carole could only be the least threatening kind of Black girl.

The only references to Blackness in Carole's life happen visually, through the infrequent presence of her dad and the even more infrequent images of her deceased mom. Halfway through season one, Carole is about to start interning with the equine veterinarian Dr. Judy. Her dad plays her a home video that shows a younger Carole playing with model horses, then getting up to greet her mom as she gets home from work. We see her mom from a distance as younger Carole runs toward her, and then the scene ends.

Carole's Blackness goes unspoken and unremarked on; it demands nothing of the other characters or the audience. In the world of the show, being a Black kid who loves ponies is exactly the same as being a white kid who loves ponies, and such sameness is not only okay, but ideal. Middle school can be a time when questions of identity come to the forefront of people's relationships, when issues of race, class, and sexuality prove their ability to bring people together or push them apart. In *The Saddle Club*'s moments of conflict and confusion, where the differences in the girls' economic backgrounds, family configurations, and racial experiences might naturally come up, we find only the shiny, equalizing veneer of girlhood. As a lighter-skinned, mixed-race kid, I interacted with many fictional characters like Carole, who modeled lessons about the kinds of spaces, ambiguity, and "acceptance" available to me if I was willing to abandon myself and other—namely, darker-skinned and less respectable—Black people. This is partly why I don't resonate with a politics of representation, a politics focused on the value of seeing "people that look like you" in media (bonus points if they're morally pure and above reproach). While I've certainly enjoyed moments of seeing Black and queer people on-screen, positive representation as an end in itself, without attending to the larger political forces that make so many of our lives untenable and so much of our media vapid and unsatisfying propaganda for the elite, does nothing to significantly change the narrative resources available to us. Too often, the outcomes of struggles for representation are media that inserts various marginalized characters as if ticking boxes on a checklist, unquestioned colorism, a simplistic prioritizing of identity markers over artistic integrity, and only the most normative and watered-down narratives being "allowed" into the mainstream. As Elaine Castillo writes in *How to Read Now*, "Representation Matters Art is late capitalism's wet dream, because it sublimates the immense hunger and desire for wide-ranging racial, sexual, gender, and economic justice into the Pepsi commercial of that justice . . . mistaking visibility for liberation."

It was cool that Carole was Black. It's part of the reason why I identified with her in ways I didn't with other
fictional horse girls. But my love for her was, and is, more
nuanced than a reductive understanding of representation
would suggest. I guess I saw myself in Carole—but more
accurately, I collaborated with Carole in finding ways to see
myself, in making meaning out of my world and the possibilities for how I could be in it. All the Saddle Club members
loved horses and dedicated much of their lives to caring
for them. But while Stevie is a funny, chaotic prankster and
Lisa is a generally anxious straight-A student, Carole's most
distinguishing personality trait is her devotion to horses—
her commitment to knowing about them, learning about
them, diagnosing them, riding them, defending them. It
is Carole who interns with Dr. Judy, Carole who has a job
exercising racehorses, and Carole who takes care of Veronica's horse when Veronica neglects to do so herself.
One could argue Carole was written as a more one-note
character than the rest of the main cast, but in her I saw
traces of my own almost desperately single-minded focus
on the things that fascinated and inspired me.

After I started riding lessons, I would read thick horse
encyclopedias and rattle off facts about horse breeds and
coat colors and equitation, happy to insert them into every
thematically unrelated conversation I was part of. Looking
back, I recognize myself as a neurodivergent kid who hadn't

yet learned the art of politely repressing one's obsessions. All I knew was that I cared about things with an intensity that could push others away, and that made the adults around me laugh awkwardly or listen for a few minutes before their eyes glazed over. As the fictional horse girl I most admired and emulated, Carole gave me hope that I could be loved in spite of and maybe because of my obsessions, that my emotional sensitivity and comfort with the nonverbal world of animals could be things that made people trust me and want to be my friend.

In *The Saddle Club* episode "A Horse of a Different Colour: Part 1," Carole returns from vacation to an uncharacteristically empty stable. While the stable is usually bustling, no one seems to be around. When she catches up with her friends, they seem consumed by mundane happenings, refusing to acknowledge Carole's hints about her upcoming birthday. She spends the week growing increasingly upset, worrying that her friends have forgotten to celebrate her. At the end of the two-part episode—perhaps to the shock of no one—Stevie and Lisa throw her a surprise birthday party, and everyone at the stable is in attendance. The three Saddle Club members seize the moment by performing a song that begins with the words "nothing without each other."

At my sixth birthday party, held in the ice-skating rink at Prospect Park in Brooklyn, I had over twenty guests. As I drew closer to middle and then high school, my social life quieted and fell away. The kids around me were beginning to figure out who they were—separating themselves into groups of various identifications, individualizing themselves from their parents, talking independently with one another through phones and the internet. The things that made my life different became barriers to connection. I was quiet and socially anxious. I had limited access to television, rendering me oblivious to pop culture. And I was homeschooled, spending the majority of my time at home or at various extracurricular activities with my mom and sister, rather than with my peers. For me, growing up as a homeschooler meant experiencing the slow creep of how abuse and social isolation can take over your days, the ways you can slowly fade into the background of other people's lives.

★   ★   ★

One of *The Saddle Club* episodes I remember most vividly is called "Gift Horse." In this episode, a horse named Delilah is pregnant and about to give birth. Dr. Judy doesn't know exactly when Delilah will go into labor, but she suspects it'll happen soon. Although the Saddle Club girls' commitment to horses is one of the show's strongest throughlines, this is a rare episode that depicts the girls as distracted. Lisa is focused on getting a part in a school play, while Stevie is spending most of her time with her old friend Tina. Carole is the only girl who stays at the stable, laser-focused on the coming birth. She's present when Delilah's water breaks, and for a while, with her friends preoccupied (and Max out on a date), she's unable at first to get in contact with anyone. She's resigned herself to being alone when Stevie and Lisa run into the stable, just in time for the birth. While Carole is upset with them at first, she quickly puts her anger aside to film the proceedings on her camcorder. The girls watch as Delilah's foal emerges from her body hooves first, covered in an amniotic sac. As he tumbles onto the hay in a rush of fluid, the Saddle Club girls remain entranced. The three of them stand outside the door of Delilah's stall, cooing at the foal's cuteness and deciding on a name for him. They're reunited, turning away from the demands of the outside world to find one another at the stable, yet again.

What strikes me about this episode is the fleshly, bodily mess of it all, the surprisingly (for a children's show) uncensored depiction of a creature's birth, replete with the foal's head emerging through the grayish membrane of amnions and placenta. Rewatching "Gift Horse," I'm also struck by the ways loneliness shapes the narrative of the episode. We see Stevie feel alienated as Tina forces her into a high-femme look that wouldn't survive a second at the barn. We see Carole alone in an empty stable at night, keeping vigil for Delilah. But these moments of isolation, of betrayal and hurt, are interrupted by the Saddle Club's dramatic and

100 percent earnest devotion to one another. Here, Carole is the one who remains steadfast, whose gaze never falters from the horse in her care. By the time I started watching *The Saddle Club*, I knew that caring way too much and having a weird amount of follow-through meant you would be left on your own sometimes. But even weirdos who care too much need people who will come back for us, who will burst in and say, *I'm sorry I left you alone, but I'm ready to help now. I was tempted by the distractions of a silly and cruel world. I wanted to be a star onstage, a pretty girl wearing makeup at the mall, but then I remembered what's important, and so I came to meet you here.*

*   *   *

Despite my social isolation, riding horses gave me opportunities to connect with others and approximate—even if only slightly—the relationships I saw in *The Saddle Club*. When I took horseback riding lessons on Long Island, most of the people I met were suburban kids whose parents drove them to the stables like the parents of the Saddle Club members' did. These kids also spent their after-school hours at the stable, riding every day, and many of them owned horses. I was a commuter, riding in with my mom and sister once a week on the Long Island Rail Road. Paying for the railroad tickets and the lessons was a financial implausibility. It was a sacrifice my parents made in service of my dreams, which became my mom's dreams too—a complicated mixture of dreams that included a childlike love for horses along with adult aspirations to a kind of upper-middle-class whiteness we could never afford, and a stubborn belief in me and my talents for which I am forever grateful.

Because of my mom's work schedule, I usually didn't go to the stable during after-school hours. But I still saw other kids on holidays, or during the rare times when I was there into the late afternoon. One of my first friends at the stable had two horses, Appaloosas with spotted coat patterns. She was slightly older than I was and had been riding much longer; I admired the way she gracefully soared over jumps during her lessons. We started talking late at night on AOL Instant Messenger, mostly chatting about horse facts or the funny things her horses would do. At another stable, I struck up a friendship with an older woman who worked as a writer at a late-night radio station. She rescued squirrels and ran an animal hospital out of her house. She would send me emails with photos and stories about the squirrels, and eventually we started to share intimacies about our lives. When I log in to my old AOL email account now, there is a folder with hundreds of emails exchanged between us over the course of several years. My mom eventually stopped me from talking to her, citing a vague mix of reasons that suggested there was no reason in particular. But for a while, this friendship was a lifeline, a place where I felt listened to and cared for in the ways I imagined the Saddle Club girls felt at Pine Hollow. My relationships with fellow horse lovers were a way I could access the kinds of interactions I had previously only seen on my television screen, where Carole, Stevie, and Lisa navigated intergenerational mentorships, casual friendships, and admiring and covetous relationships with older riders.

*   *   *

Even though *The Saddle Club* includes boys, they are very obviously not the point. Kristi's many and fleeting crushes are a running gag, and each of the Saddle Club members kisses a boy at least once over the course of the show. By the end of season two, Stevie has a kind-of boyfriend named Phil. But the show's most pressing emotional concerns hinge on a social world of girls and their desires, their ambitions and petty rivalries, their knowledge, their playfulness, their sense of justice and love. I loved horse girls before I knew I was queer, and before I knew I wasn't a girl. But *The Saddle Club* gave me one of my most enduring childhood models for networks of care centered on girls and women, horses and dogs, and the occasional guinea pig. It was a form of the social that stretched boundaries between species and the demands of heterosexuality, prefiguring the kinds of relationships—with my friends and mentors, with the living world—that structure my life today.

In one of the scenes from the episode "Horse's Keeper," the Saddle Club girls convene in the hayloft to discuss the urgent issue of Veronica selling her horse. The three of them lay intertwined on the hay bales, with Carole's head resting on Lisa, and Stevie hanging upside down with her legs draped over the other two. Even now, that easy, casual image of physical intimacy remains highlighted in my mind. I remember looking at it with an amorphous yearning—a yearning for the everyday romance of friendship, for the kinds of relationships where it felt natural and organic to lay your head on your friend's lap or your legs on a friend's legs, to have the weight of you supported by someone who loves you. In *Modest_Witness@Second_Millennium. FemaleMan_Meets_OncoMouse: Feminism and Technoscience*, feminist science and technology scholar Donna Haraway writes, "I am sick to death of bonding through kinship and 'the family,' and I long for models of solidarity and human unity and difference rooted in friendship, work, partially shared purposes, intractable collective pain, inescapable mortality, and persistent hope." The world of *The Saddle Club* is in many ways presented as a carefully depoliticized one. But it was also one of the first stories that showed me what it could look like to create family-like bonds outside the nuclear family unit, to form connections out of choice rather than happenstance or obligation.*

Watching *The Saddle Club* again in preparation for writing this essay, I was struck by the amount of misfortune that plagued Pine Hollow—the horses that died or became gravely ill or were suspected of being gravely ill, the horses that were threatened with being put down or sold if they didn't get better at their jobs, the near-death accidents, the fire that broke out in the stable, the horse that had to be euthanized after he broke his leg going over a jump. I had remembered the show as a happy one, but I think that's because I remembered it as a show about belonging. And I would say, all these years later, that it is. It's a show about your people coming to gather you, again and again, and how this gathering makes it possible to get up each day and brave the heartbreaks. I am forever indebted to Carole, the token Black girl of Pine Hollow. I hope that wherever Carole is, she continues to be someone who remains and remembers and is held close in that remembering, knowing there are folks who will wait up with her through the night.

---

* It's worth noting that these early models of intimacy (including the scene in the hayloft) also diverge in many ways from the kinds of relationships I have today. As I discuss in the essay, *The Saddle Club* presented a color-blind universe, one in which a Black girl could have a seemingly all-white social circle with apparently no psychic or emotional damage. As I got older, I held on to the lessons of loyalty and intimacy modeled by *The Saddle Club*, while creating a social world centered on love and kinship with other people of color.

A 1996 copy of a Saddle Club book
with Carole on the cover.

HORSE OF THE DIVINE

*A*n *ancestor altar doesn't have to be fancy. It can be located on a bedside table, in a spot under a nearby tree, in a corner of the kitchen. Just try to make sure you have some things representing the elements. A glass of water, a white candle. Incense for smoke, and so on. Maybe a smooth rock you found on a walk one day. Maybe a photo of someone who came before you, someone you claim as predecessor. This is what I learned from my teachers—the parents and artists and researchers and podcast hosts and authors and diviners who guided me through connection to West African–based spiritual practices. Sometimes I think I believe in the altar, in the posture of devotional practice, more than any literary form. An altar can be an essay too. Here are some offerings.*

★ This description of an altar is informed by teachings from spiritual educators and scholars like Juju Bae and Ehime Ora, who seek to make West African–originated spiritual traditions more accessible to Black people throughout the diaspora. While these basic altar elements can be found throughout many traditions, there are extensive and nuanced differences between altars in practices such as Santería, Ifá, Vodou, Candomblé, and Palo Mayombe, to name a few.

altar table: the foundation

In the Nigerian Yoruba religion, Shango is an orisha of thunder and lightning, justice and virility. He is a deity with swagger, a dancing spirit who summons storms with double-headed bata drums. As the artist Tiona Nekkia McClodden writes, one might consider Shango "the Rico Suave of the Orisha." Before he became a deity, Shango was a seventeenth-century king of the famed Oyo Empire, located in present-day Benin and Western Nigeria. As the empire's wealth grew, its leaders invested in the import of horses. Oyo became known for its armed cavalry, which enabled the empire to expand far beyond the reaches of neighboring kingdoms and establish trade on the Atlantic coast. Shango was an expert equestrian and military leader. In praise songs celebrating him, he was said to have a stable of ten thousand horses.

Orisha are Yoruba deities sent by the creator Olodumare to help humans survive on earth. They often preside over specific landforms and elements, residing in rivers, forests, mountains, streams, the ocean, the wind. There are countless orisha, with some accounts listing over a thousand. The orisha are fallible deities, not above pettiness, arrogance, and deceit. In myths about the orisha, they fight and love as humans do—with great passion and great flaws. Exceptional humans can become orisha after death. And so it was that the king of the Oyo Empire became the deity Shango.

Like his human self, the orisha Shango also rides a horse. On his altars and shrines, he is honored by elesin Shango—carved wood and ivory sculptures depicting him on horseback. In many of these sculptures, Shango is disproportionately large, several times taller than his horse. Viewed from afar, the elesin Shango can appear to represent a single towering being, traveling on four short legs. Rather than simply being a mount, Shango's horse is often presented as an embodiment of his physical prowess and fierce nature. In some ways, the horse can be seen as simply an extension of the deity himself; riding is one manifestation of how he interacts with the world. As a praise song for Shango says, "Fire in the eye / fire in the mouth / fire on the roof / You ride fire like a horse."

glass of water: clear channel to the spirits

Tiona Nekkia McClodden's video installation *I prayed to the wrong god for you* documents her journey of connection with Shango, featuring a retired racehorse as an embodiment of the deity's horse. Tiona is a priestess in the Afro-Caribbean religion of Santería, a syncretic practice that blends elements of Roman Catholicism with the Yoruba divinatory tradition of Ifá. Her deepening relationship with Shango took her to Pennsylvania; Maine; Havana, Cuba; a shrine in Ibadan, Nigeria; and a horse stable in upstate New York, charting a transatlantic geography of ritual and prayer. Tiona made six tools for Shango: the double-sided axe he is most commonly associated with, along with a single-sided axe, a hatchet, two knives, and an arrow. Constructed in Maine and sanded in Havana before traveling to Ibadan, the installation's material objects reflect the diasporic circulation of Shango himself: an orisha who survived the Middle Passage along with the enslaved Africans who prayed to him, disembarking with his horse in the New World.

In a conversation in *Art in America*, McClodden and art historian Genevieve Hyacinthe discuss horse imagery in Black diasporic spiritual practices. Hyacinthe mentions fifteenth-century Malian sculptures of "human bodies melting into the bodies of horses, suggesting that they are one." Where does the human end and the horse begin? Where are the boundaries between the material world and the spirit world, between divinities and the beings they ride? In the elesin Shango, the Malian sculptures, and the mythology of the orisha themselves is a fluidity of form and meaning that defies colonial logics, proposing different answers to the familiar question of what a body can be.

incense: smoke spirals, transformation

In Haitian vodou ceremonies, people often become possessed by deities known as lwa, entering into trance states as the spirits move through them. When this happens, it is said that the worshippers are being mounted by the lwa, that they have become horses for the divine.

In *Tell My Horse: Voodoo and Life in Haiti and Jamaica,* Zora Neale Hurston writes of her ethnographic travels studying spiritual life on the two Caribbean islands. Describing her observation of vodou practice, Hurston tells stories of mounted peasants who mock wealthy people in public and berate local officials to their faces, as the lwa talk through their mouths. Hurston speculates that while some of the mountings must be genuine, others are surely feigned as an excuse for expressing resentment. Being a horse of the lwa means existing in a temporary space where everyday people can subvert the limits of class, claiming the right to speak down to their oppressors. These moments of rupture are the origin of the Haitian saying "Tell my horse." Hurston writes that the proverb is used as a "blind for self-expression," a way of invoking the figure of the horse to justify saying the unsayable.

When someone is ridden by a lwa, the deity has a say in how the person inhabits their human form. Baron Samedi, the loa (lwa) of the dead, is sometimes depicted as an effeminate man, a trans person, or a bisexual person. Hurston writes that when Baron Samedi mounts his devotees, he takes pleasure in having them cross-dress. "Often the men, in addition to wearing female clothes, thrust a calabash up under their skirts to simulate pregnancy. Women put on men's coats and prance about with a stick between their legs to imitate the male sex organs." To be a horse of the lwa means having a gateway to the otherwise. It means being temporarily freed from the constrictions of daily life, accountable only to the clear-eyed morality of the gods.

white votive candle: flame, flickering

Hurston also visited the Accompong Maroons in Jamaica, a community of rural people descended from escaped slaves who built strongholds in the hills of Cockpit Country during the seventeenth century. One of the stories the Maroons told her was that of the ghostly being known as the three-leg-horse duppy.

They say the three-leg-horse duppy will follow you and chase you, especially between the hours of one and four in the morning. They say only women are scared of the three-leg-horse, but there's no reason for the fright; he's just a creature looking for some fun. They say he shows up around Christmas, joining in the masquerades and the merriment, dressing himself up in costume disguise just like everyone else. The three-leg-horse duppy is ridden by the Whooping Boy, a former cowherd whose voice precedes him as he rides through the night.

Duppies are ghost things, spirits who sometimes take the form of living beings, haunted remembrances. Duppies can be playful or violent, benevolent or terrifying by turns. Duppy walk, duppy talk, duppy will try to catch you unawares. Duppy know who fi frighten and who fi tell good night—in other words, they can recognize the spiritually vulnerable, know who might be due for a visitation.

Hurston concluded the three-leg-horse was a remnant of a West African puberty rite and sexual symbol. Others believe the three-leg-horse and the Whooping Boy are references to events from plantation slavery. It's true that our ghost stories often reflect the terrors that echo throughout our lives, but linear explanations feel disrespectful here. As much as the three-leg-horse and other duppies may be tied to historical rememberings, they are their own realities—to know the duppy is to have an understanding of the world that can't fully be explained in sociological terms.

If being mounted by a spirit is about abandoning the idea of a distinct self, dealing with duppy business is about figuring out how to shield yourself from a mysterious entity. Both practices deal with porousness—an acknowledgment that spirits can touch us, shape us, take hold of us in ways we can't anticipate or control. Here is how you can try to protect yourself from duppies: Sprinkle salt, rice, or peas on the ground. Avoid the planting of almond trees too close to the home. Drink Spirit Weed tea. Throw dried peas in the grave while burying a body. Put the limb of a cotton tree on top of the coffin. Plant sweet basil. Burn cow shit. Drop stones behind you as you walk in the dark. These are some of the ways we attempt to negotiate our hauntings, making peace with our spirits and our ghosts, and all that they will ask of us.

flowers: an offering of beauty, a celebration

The horse-headed woman sits with a thick green mane flowing over her shoulder. She wears a long black dress, and a sharp blade protrudes from her upper back. She has dark brown hands clasped in her lap, a pair of white horns on her head, and testicles where we might otherwise expect a nose. Between the horns sits the round red figure of Elegua, orisha of the crossroads.

In the 1940s, Cuban painter Wifredo Lam began a series of pieces depicting *femme cheval*, or horse-headed women. Born in 1902, Lam grew up in the largely Chinese Cuban community of Sagua la Grande. His childhood was shaped by his Afro-Cuban godmother Mantonica Wilson, a Shango priestess who practiced Santería and was a noted community healer. Lam traveled to France in his twenties and become influenced by the surrealism and cubism of contemporaries like André Breton and Picasso. During this time, he also became friends with anticolonial thinkers like Martinican poet Aimé Césaire. When Lam returned to Cuba in 1941, the country was experiencing massive amounts of poverty created by US intervention. After the United States formally withdrew from Cuba following the Spanish-American War, it had established a military base at Guantanamo Bay and continued a de facto occupation of the island. During the Prohibition era, Americans flocked to Cuba for cheap liquor, leading to an expansion of an extractive tourist industry. It was within this context that Lam committed to uplifting Afro-Cuban culture and history through his work, writing, "I decided that my painting would never be the equivalent of that pseudo-Cuban music for nightclubs. . . . I wanted with all my heart to paint the drama of my country, but by thoroughly expressing the Negro spirit."

Lam's horse-headed women are imposing figures, erect in posture and often armed or featuring sharp appendages. Many have long hair, rounded breasts, and curves, contrasting sharply with the angular, cubist-inspired aspects of their bodies. Referencing the concept of a worshipper mounted by spirit, the horse-headed women embody Lam's project of creating a distinctly Afro-Cuban modernism.

Lam was part of the Vanguardia movement, a group of Cuban artists active in the 1930s and 1940s whose work drew from cubism, surrealism, and Mexican muralism. These artists, including painters Mario Carreño, Amelia Peláez, and Carlos Enríquez Gómez, destabilized the more conservative practices of portraiture and landscape painting that had dominated Cuban art school pedagogy. Many of their works engaged with Afro-Cuban life—in Carlos Enríquez Gómez's 1933 *Virgen del Cobre*, the painter depicted Cuba's Catholic patron saint as the orisha Ochun. However, unlike many of his contemporaries, Wifredo Lam's work brings the viewer directly into the messy, unpredictable space of ritual and ceremony. In contrast to the serene beauty of Enríquez's Ochun, Lam's horse-headed women have bodies that are morphing and dissembling, sprouting candles and horns, sporting genitalia in surprising places, adorned with spikes and knives. In his *femme cheval* paintings, Lam proposes a vision of portraiture that is not about prettiness, or legibility, but rather about the chaotic, powerful, and sometimes dangerous work of spiritual transformation.

In addition to the portraits, the figure of the horse-headed woman also appears in Lam's most famous work, *La Jungla* (The Jungle). *La Jungla* portrays four figures against a backdrop of sugarcane stalks, referencing the sugarcane plantations worked by slaves in Cuba for centuries. The figures' faces are reminiscent of African masks, their bodies a surreal and tangled assemblage of limbs, buttocks, breasts. To the far left of the painting is a horse-headed woman. Her features mirror those of the other *femme cheval*, and she stands with one hand against a piece of sugarcane. A figure of Elegua floats near her feet. *La Jungla* places the horse-headed woman in historical context, showing how Santería emerged from the conditions of chattel slavery. The blade extending from the *femme cheval*'s back was forged in struggle. Carrying weapons like Shango, shifting into wild and indecipherable forms like a devotee possessed, she invites us into the untranslatable meeting place of the horse, the human, and the divine.

ceremony

I have rewritten this many times, and I think I am reaching the limit of what words can do here. But if you want to and you can, I invite you to sit with me awhile, at the feet of something that beckons us away from who we know ourselves to be. Sit with me here as we feel our selves dissolve, novel shapes emerging from under our skins, knives and machetes where once there were hands and spines. Sit with me here as we shudder and shake and a new breath fills our lungs, until we are no longer sitting but dancing, our hooves resounding against the ground. Be with me by the ocean, in the cane fields, in the heart of the fire, at the crossroads, in the hills, behind the duppy's back. Shout with a voice you don't recognize but is now your own.

Yorùbá, *Figure of Shango on Horseback*, early twentieth
century. Wood, pigment,
40 × 14½ × 9 in. (101.6 × 36.8 × 22.9 cm).

Wifredo Lam, *Je Suis*, 1949, oil on canvas,
48.9 × 43.1 in. (124.2 × 109.5 cm).

BECOMING ANIMAL

I.

Have I ever been mounted? That's between me and the spirits, the hauntings and half directives that live like murmurs in my body. I know I've mounted you because I've felt you beneath me, writhing into new forms, flesh creatures in the moments between hours.

When I fuck you sometimes I feel myself becoming animal, pushing past the ill-fitting skins that follow me into bed. I told you I wanted to be a cat with long silver claws toying with their prey. I told you I wanted to be your pup. When you wear a mask do you become less human to me? Does it feel easier to ruin you? When I top you until I turn animal, or shed my human skin to reach the parts of me that want to be brutal, does it feel easier to look in my eyes afterward?

II.

look in my eyes

The material culture of BDSM is, in many ways, a masquerade of a European gentleman with his stable of horses—leather, whips, bits and bridles. Tall boots, harnesses. Imagine it—the unspoken perversities that made him. The horrors of the colonies, the erotic undersides of a metropole drenched in blood. It's always fascinated me how parts of the (white) kink community could engage in master/slave play for decades without any critical thought about the historical implications of those roles. I know it's because the Middle Passage made them too. Even as descriptors of a relationship that predated the New World, would those words hold the same weight if not for transatlantic slavery? Would they carry the same (twisted) pleasures?

III.

twisted pleasure

In Tschabalala Self's 2018 piece *Horse*, two paper-collaged figures are presented side by side, one penetrating the other with a purple dick. The penetrated figure stands in a distorted side profile, with one of their breasts protruding while the other points toward the viewer. Their face, like their one visible foot, is deep purple, with mismatched eyes and eyebrows, and a velvety cheetah-print turban is wrapped on their head. The penetrating figure wears a suit jacket, and their body seems to end at their genitals. One purple hand is wrapped around the other's waist.

There is a matter-of-factness that takes me aback every time I look at this piece. Maybe the figures have been disturbed while engaging in an intimate act, or maybe they are just presenting their bodies, in one configuration of what bodies can do with and for each other. They are in a position that some may associate with pleasure, but the feeling here isn't one of raucous desire or joy. Their position suggests movement, but they are arrested in time rather than in active motion. Meeting their gazes, I find myself waiting to be told something, to be given an explanation. I grasp for meaning, looking for the contours of shame or shock I have been conditioned to see. But these figures are simply as they

Tschabalala Self, *Horse*, 2018, flashe (vinyl emulsion paint), gouache, acrylic paint, oil paint, thread, faux fur, digitally printed canvas, and fabric on canvas, 84 × 72 in.

are, doing with their bodies as they must or as they will, and that is all the information I deserve to know.

There is no horse in *Horse*, at least not in the ways we might expect. But the language of riding—and being ridden—is also a language of sex, used to describe physical positions and the power dynamics that accompany them. The language of riding and being ridden is an animal vocabulary, inherently reminding us of the slippery boundaries between "animal" and "human," the ways the figure of the beast haunts our intimate lives.

IV.

the figure of the beast

In a roundtable discussion published in *The New Inquiry* called "Top or Bottom: How Do We Desire?," the writers Billy-Ray Belcourt, Kay Gabriel, and George Dust talk about the ways that racialized categories of animal and human haunt queer sexual culture.* As Belcourt, Gabriel, and Dust discuss, there's a robust tradition of white liberals who feel guilty about racism seeking to rid themselves of complicity. One manifestation of this is the white fantasy of being sexually dominated by Black and brown people—in other words, making the oppressed occupy the position of the (supposed) aggressor, the "animal." By submitting to a person of color, they can feel they are performing a kind of penance, a kind of reparative power reversal that still ultimately dehumanizes their sexual partner. Dust re-

---

* George Dust, who participated in the "Top or Bottom: How Do We Desire?" roundtable, has since been revealed to be an online persona created by the writer Jackie Ess. Ess is a trans writer and the author of the novel *Darryl*, a book about cuckolding, marriage, sexuality, and Oregon, among other things. After learning of the Jackie Ess / George Dust situation, I decided to keep Dust's quotes in this essay. While Dust may have been a satirical persona, the observations they make in *The New Inquiry* roundtable are insightful, ring true to my own experiences and that of many other queer people I have spoken with, and are in conversation with a robust critical tradition of thinkers investigating the colonial constructions of animal/human categories.

calls a passage in writer Christian Maurel's text *The Screwball Asses*, in which Maurel describes the sexual behavior of young white French queers who desire to be fucked by Arab people. "What the young gay man says to the Arab is still an avowal of guilt: 'The bourgeoisie exploits you, my father exploits you, so fuck me!' . . . Class struggle, class masochism, what hides behind this artificial appropriation of the primitive?" By asking or fantasizing about being dominated by Black and brown people, white people beg to be absolved for their ancestral sins. At the same time, they are projecting their fears of the nonhuman—their fears about what colonial brutality has made of them—onto another.

The roles of top and bottom don't neatly map onto an established order of things. Tops can be submissive; bottoms can be calling the shots. And in some ways, the definition of "top" in this roundtable is inflected by a cis gay male perspective on the power dynamics of penetration. In a book not structured around the experience of gay men, the directive spoken by Christian Maurel's character could also be heard as: *Dom(me) me. Tie me up. Tell me how I can be yours.*

Regardless, I believe the basic premise put forth by Belcourt, Gabriel, and Dust still stands: that the white yearning to be sexually dominated by the colonized is a way of displacing responsibility, a way of creating a moral high ground that establishes the dominant person as animal, with all the connotations such words carry in a colonial context. As Gabriel says, "I'll suggest that top/bottom mirrors the animal/human distinction, that it's a gradient of dehumanization. The top isn't afforded innocence or subjectivity."

V.

innocence

I must confess that sometimes I fear I've done it wrong.

VI.

wrong

To become animal is to place yourself beyond redemption, beyond the pale (excuse the pun) of the law. In my practice of dominance, I worry that I've made myself less worthy of care. That I've turned myself into something definitionally unable to be harmed. The "perfect victim" is passive and pure, a desireless body made prey to the violent desires of another. What happens when the victim claims hunger and want? What happens when the dominating admits hunger for care?

VII.

hunger and want

In my worry and self-consciousness, in my fear that I've *done it wrong*, I find myself consumed by what you might think. You and you. Despite my best intentions, I still have an intuitive, reactionary response to the dehumanization Gabriel et al. speak of, the relentless association between Black people and the animal. And that is to contort myself into the shape of the colonial human. To resist animality at every turn, to keep my desires quiet and unobtrusive, to become obsessed with proving my capacity for innocence.

In many of my favorite Tschabalala Self pieces, her collaged figures have no use for bodily coherence. Their faces, breasts, and limbs exist in mismatched glory, sliding between 2D and 3D, calling us into unknown geometries. In *For the Gods*, a figure bends backward, supported on one mottled purple leg, while a yellow hand and orange foot are flung upward toward the heavens—a prayer, perhaps. In *Floor Dance*, a figure with four arms does a wide grand jeté, each hand poised in classical elegance. I remember walking into the New Museum in 2017 and seeing *Floor Dance* on the wall. My first thought: *Let's play.*

In order to create new languages for the body, an erotics

unfettered by the geographies of the plantation—its animal-human relations, its definitions of the monstrous—we must rid ourselves of our fear of the animal. This is what Self's work reminds me: that there is levity in the ways we can slip out of our given skins, mischief in the ways we can challenge the meanings imposed upon our forms. We mount and are mounted, losing our received names and becoming beasts for one another. There is no redemption here, and no Human either.

WORKING ANIMALS

All horses, save for wild ones, are workhorses, and all workhorses, like all human workers, are survivors of the world they build and from which they are cast aside.

—David Grundy

Slavery's archival footprint is a ledger system that placed black humans, horses, cattle, and household items all on the same bill of purchase. This ledger's biopolitical arithmetic—its calculation of humanity—dislocated, depersonalized, and collapsed difference, except in the area of market value.

—Zakiyyah Iman Jackson

In August 1781, a British slave ship called the *Zong* departed Accra, Ghana, for the island of Jamaica, carrying 442 enslaved Africans on board. By November, due to the incompetence and mismanagement of the crew, the ship had sailed off course, missing Jamaica by several hundred miles. Over sixty Africans had already died from disease or malnutrition. Faced with the prospect of losing money due to this lost human cargo and poor navigation, the crew decided to make an insurance claim. They massacred more than 140 Africans over the course of several days, throwing them overboard into the Atlantic. When the ship's crew reached Jamaica, they appealed to their insurance company to compensate them for the people they had murdered, claiming that insufficient water supplies on the ship had made it necessary to carry out such a plan.

The case was tried in London before Chief Justice Lord Mansfield, and a jury ruled in favor of the ship's owners. After new evidence emerged (including proof that an abundant 1,900 liters of water had still been aboard the ship when it reached Jamaica), Mansfield called for a retrial that never occurred. Summarizing the case, Mansfield said the jury had to consider "whether [the mass murder arose] [. . .] from necessity[,] for they had no doubt (tho' it shocks one very much) the Case of Slaves was the same as if Horses had been thrown over board." Later in his remarks, he said again that the insurers were obligated to pay for slaves killed in uprisings "just as if Horses were kill'd," but did not have to pay for slaves, or horses, who died natural deaths. In a case that garnered widespread media attention and galvanized the British abolitionist movement, it would be easy for Mansfield's remarks to go overlooked, simply another example of the dehumanization of the murdered Africans. However, his comments point to a central underpinning of transatlantic slavery: the relationships between enslaved Africans and working animals like horses, created through colonial ideology and through the economic geographies of the plantation. In the callousness of its economic logic, Mansfield's comments lay bare the ways anti-Blackness and plantation slavery made animals of all laboring bodies.

★ ★ ★

Abolitionist and writer Frederick Douglass, in his 1845 autobiography, writes of a property inventory that took place at a plantation where he was enslaved as a child. "We were all ranked together at the valuation. Men and women, old and young, married and single, were ranked with horses, sheep, and swine." Throughout Douglass's autobiography, and many other nineteenth-century slave narratives, Black people and four-legged animals were categorized together in the ledgers of slaveholders as assets and living engines of the plantation economy.

At the same time as slavery created a totalizing category of those who labored to produce value for the slave owner, horses occupied a fluid role in the hierarchies of plantation society. Plantation overseers rode horses in order to move through rows of crops, surveying and surveilling enslaved people as they worked. Slave patrollers rode horses, relying on the speed and acuity of their mounts in order to detect those who sought to escape. And slave owners relied on horses to establish their position as propertied men, literally elevated above those who struggled and labored on the ground. The horse, conscripted into various forms of work by those in power, could be a vehicle of terror as well as a downtrodden farm animal. And so while it's crucial to see the ways Black people and horses experienced shared conditions and shared violences, the archives also remind us of the ways horses could be set apart from humans and used as tools of oppression. In *River of Dark Dreams*, historian Walter Johnson writes that "the sound of an approaching horse was a fearful portent" to escaping slaves, a way for slave owners to "command the landscape" and assert their control over the people they were said to own.

★   ★   ★

In Boots Riley's 2018 movie *Sorry to Bother You*, a young Black man named Cassius "Cash" Green is struggling to make ends meet in Oakland. He's living in his uncle's garage with his girlfriend, Detroit, and he's about to get kicked out. He gets hired to work for a telemarketing company called Regalview, where his job is to sit in a cubicle all day and make cold calls to potential clients while making sure to STTS, or Stick to the Script. He's doing badly with sales until an older Black man tells him to use his white voice, a voice that is nasal, breezy, unburdened. When Cash follows his co-worker's advice, he starts closing deals left and right, ascending to the elite rank of Power Caller.

While working for Regalview, Cash realizes the company sells arms and cheap labor from the corporation WorryFree. WorryFree has been advertising what they call a groundbreaking new arrangement: a kind of glorified worker's camp where employees are given bunk beds in overcrowded rooms and promised guaranteed housing, food, and a job. Like many "guaranteed" and "free" things under capitalism, the strings attached are obviously too numerous to count. At a company party, WorryFree's CEO, Steve Lift, pulls Cash into his office and begins playing him a video. When Cash leaves to the bathroom, he hears a voice calling for help in one of the stalls. Opening it, he sees a body lying chained to the floor in front of him. The body has the head of a horse and a muscular, vaguely human form, with appendages that are somewhere between hands, feet, and hooves. The figure continues begging for

Cash's help. As more of these horse-human forms emerge from behind bathroom stalls, Cash runs. When he confronts Lift, the CEO forces him to finish the video, which turns out to be an infomercial of sorts. The video explains that WorryFree is developing a drug to turn humans into even better workers by transforming them into hybrid equine bodies—Equisapiens. The upbeat narrator's voice identifies this project as a natural next step in human development, an extension of the self-betterment impulse that drives us to study, exercise, and use tools. To the narrator, and to Lift, this is simply a logical way for companies to make more profit and have better workers. When they finish the video, Lift seems relieved to have his impeccable reasoning clarified. "I just didn't want you to think I was crazy, that I was doing this for no reason," he tells Cash. "This isn't irrational."

To thrive at Regalview, Cash has to alter his voice by creating a telephone avatar, a fiction that conjures an image of a body and a person that doesn't exist. In order to make money to survive, he must be willing to physically contort himself into something that will be valuable to his bosses. The Equisapiens are the monstrous, logical extension of this—humans whose bodies have been completely transformed in the service of capital. In an interview with *Vulture*, filmmaker Riley explained his choice to include the Equisapiens. "I was looking for something that also had to do with the way that I feel capitalism is making us right now, which is to be more efficient monsters, right? . . . So why horses? We think of a horse as something that's for work. It's in our language—horsepower."

*　　*　　*

In 1873, Frederick Douglass gave a speech titled "Agriculture and Black Progress" to recently freed Black farmers at the Third Annual Fair of the Colored Agricultural and Mechanical Association. In this speech, he gave advice on how his listeners might establish themselves in business and life, covering topics like caring for one's tools and maintaining soil health. Addressing the weighty topic of how to build thriving Black communities after centuries of chattel slavery, Douglass's remarks ranged from the broadly theoretical to the domestic and mundane—for example, the need to stock the woodpile and put a well near the house, so that one's wife wouldn't have to travel an unpleasant distance for household duties.

In his reflections on the relations between slaves and animals on the plantation, one of Douglass's central concerns was putting forth a vision of changed relations between Black agrarians and the animals who worked with them. He acknowledged that slavery had produced a system of mistreatment of agricultural working animals and entreated the audience to do things differently in their new lives, to refrain from flogging and other unkindnesses. He told them that "it should be the study of every farmer to make his horse his companion and friend," stating that "a horse is in many respects like a man. He has the five senses, and has memory, affection, and reason." It's striking that in a speech about Black farmers establishing the terms of their lives after slavery, Douglass spent so much time talking about nonhuman animals. In the speech, he talked about the fact that Black people were functioning with knowledge systems inherited from white people and emphasized the imperative to "prove that we can better our own condition." Douglass's vision of Black people's betterment did not end at human communities but included a view of the interdependent networks of living beings whose survival was inextricably bound with one another. In order to emerge from the long shadow of slavery and create new ways of being, he believed it was necessary to reimagine the ways humans and animals related to one another.

When I read Douglass's speech, what stands out to me is the way that labor is a crucial aspect of the relational practices he puts forth. What he proposes is essentially an ethics of solidarity between laboring beings, between farmers and the animals who work beside them in the field. A practice of friendship between beings who, to quote Riley, were seen as "something that's for work." Douglass's proposal is also a reclamation of what work could mean and do for Black people after slavery, recasting agricultural work as a possible site of self-governance, part of an expansive ecological vision of the world that people and animals could make. This is not to glorify what it means to be a worker—particularly a Black worker—under capitalism. To be a Black farmer in the Reconstruction South often meant being in a constant cycle of· debt and poverty, working land without the proper tools or resources to do so, undergoing violence from white landowners and Klan members. But within the intolerable conditions of exploited labor, it is only by looking beyond ourselves, toward the workers of any species that toil alongside us, that we can begin to understand and to change the privations that shape our lives.

*   *   *

After learning about the Equisapiens, Cash gives up being a Power Caller and reconciles with the union organizer friends he had turned his back on. In order to air footage of the Equisapiens, he goes on a reality TV show where contestants endure physical pain and humiliation in order to win cash prizes. When he wins, he urges the showrunners to play the video of the Equisapiens calling for help from the bathroom. Then he does the rounds of daytime television talk shows, giving interviews about the urgent need to stop the horrors of WorryFree. At the same time, the government and mainstream media are applauding Worry-Free for their innovation, and if people find this news unsettling, most have chosen to ignore it. At a protest Cash and his friends organize against Regalview, a police officer knocks him unconscious with a baton and throws him in the back of a van. When he comes to, he watches through a window as a group of Equisapiens hijacks a truck, subdues several police officers, and runs toward the van, breaking down the back doors and freeing him. When Cash gets out of the van, he tries to thank the Equisapiens in the kind of obnoxiously slow, halting English that Americans have been known to use with nonfluent speakers. "Dude, I'm from East Oakland," one of the Equisapiens says. "Talk regular." Cash's instinct on first seeing the Equisapiens had been to run away, to plead for them not to touch him. I mean, no judgment. I wouldn't want to have a casual hang with horse-human hybrids I just found in a bathroom. But even as Cash continues to see himself as different from the Equisapiens, doubting their abilities to understand him when he speaks, he is reminded that the distance between him and the other Black guy from Oakland who was turned into a horse is not as large as he might think.

By the end of the film, Cash is back in his converted garage with Detroit. He stumbles to the floor, heaving with exertion. When he looks up at Detroit, his face has started to transform into that of a horse. In the film's final scenes, Cash breaks into Lift's house with a herd of other Equisapiens behind him.

Throughout the film, Cash is on the run: from poverty and eviction, from the sinister undersides of Regalview and WorryFree, from the Black voice and the rabble-rousing friends who are holding him back from ascending to a financially stable, bourgeois life, and from the specter of the Equisapien that he is terrified to become. As he falls apart, becoming unmade by his own doomed efforts to succeed within Regalview, he is forced to confront each of the things he is trying to run from. After he has resigned himself to his garage apartment and relinquished his Power Caller lifestyle, it seems like he has escaped becoming a horse creature. But eventually the horse body comes for him too, because there's nowhere to hide from the machinations of WorryFree and the system that created it. And in the end, horrified as he may be by what his body is becoming, as much as he may want to hang on to his tenuous identity as a human, he must turn toward his Equisapien comrades in order to defy Lift's power.

To form cross-species solidarities between workers is to challenge the logic of the ledger, to undermine a system that views all laborers—human and animal alike—as replaceable and exploitable. To make of one's horse a "companion and friend" is, as Douglass tells us, a necessary step toward sustaining life that exists beyond the brutal confines of slavery and European colonization. By turning toward the monstrous and creaturely figure of the animal, we recognize the ways we have been shaped by the demands of capitalism, the ways our bodies might work together in unison on a picket line or in a siege of a CEO's property or on the land of a free Black community to insist on the urgent need to make a world we can survive.

EQUESTRIAN CHIC

Two teams of white men on horseback emerge from behind the camera's view, holding wooden mallets extended toward the sky. They wear white riding pants and helmets, crisp black boots. One team wears white polo shirts, and the other wears navy blue. They canter forward, and the camera's viewpoint changes, with the men now riding toward the camera in a tight-knit throng. "Polo isn't just a game," a narrator declares over a driving orchestral score. "It's a way of life." From different angles, we see the riders swing their mallets toward the ground as their horses gallop forward in an unbroken rhythm. Close-ups of the horses moving past, mirroring the single-mindedness and muscularity of the riders. At one point, two horses from opposing teams laterally collide, unsteadied for a moment before quickly finding their footing. Their riders keep their mallets in the air, poised for the advantageous moment, for possession of the ball, for victory. The camera focuses in on a blue-shirted rider with a mallet raised above his head. The lens zooms out until the rider is pictured on the front of a glass perfume bottle with a gold cap. The image transforms into the gold Ralph Lauren logo of a horse and rider in the same position, and the words "Polo by Ralph Lauren" appear at the bottom of the screen as the narrator reads them out. The image then zooms out further, showing the perfume bottle lying in the hay. It's surrounded by the accoutrements of a polo competitor: a brown leather saddle, wooden mallet, helmet, ball, and blue duffel bag with elegant leather detailing. "This generously sized polo bag," the narrator continues. "Yours for just twenty dollars with any seventeen-dollar purchase."

This 1986 advertisement for the clothing and lifestyle brand Polo Ralph Lauren regularly appeared on televisions across the United States. Since its launch in 1968, Polo Ralph Lauren has sold a vision of old-money white luxury: country clubs and tennis courts, polo matches and yachts. The brand champions the kind of unmarked WASPy elegance that has been constructed and exported as synonymous with the American Dream: the allure of beauty without context, accumulation without effort, wealth without a hint of the disenfranchisement that made such abundance possible. But in the 1980s, an unlikely group of Black and brown youth in Brooklyn claimed Polo Ralph Lauren as their own. The Lo Lifes hailed from working-class neighborhoods like Ca-

narsie and Brownsville, Crown Heights and Bed-Stuy. Young
and broke, they found money where they could. Sometimes
this meant breaking into jewelry stores or clothing outlets
throughout Manhattan. However, as Polo Ralph Lauren
grew in prominence, their activities found a new point of focus. The Lo Lifes (named after the "Lo" in the brand's name)
developed elaborate systems for shoplifting clothes from
Polo Ralph Lauren stores in Manhattan, emptying the racks
under the noses of security guards and the general public.
They would then resell these clothes in Brooklyn, making
the brand something to be coveted, desired, and fought over.

In an interview with *The Fader*, Rack-Lo, one of the Lo
Lifes' founding members, talked about the group's origins.
He described how the Lo Lifes formed from groups in two
Brooklyn neighborhoods: the Ralphie's Kids from St. John's
and Utica, and the United Shoplifters Association from
Brownsville. When asked about the reasons behind the
group's interest in Polo Ralph Lauren, Rack-Lo said, "It represented a whole different lifestyle from what we were used
to in Brownsville and in Crown Heights. . . . It inspired us to
pursue those things: to go yachting, to be on Fifth Avenue, to
be a part of the rich and the elite." In many ways, the daily
realities of Lo Life members were incongruent with the fever
dreams sold to them by Polo Ralph Lauren. I doubt they all
believed they would transform themselves into the country
club WASPs of the Polo ads, that by wearing a certain shirt

or pair of shoes they could lay claim to the forms of power that had been systematically denied them. Many former Lo Lifes describe their relationship with Polo as one of economic pragmatism, of recognizing a fantasy and repurposing it for their own ends. While they may have begun their pursuit of Polo out of a sense of aspiration and a desire to access some of the wealth represented by the brand, they ended up shaping the trajectory of Polo for generations to come.

Polo "boosters"—those who made an art out of stealing the brand's clothing from stores—became an integral force in shaping the brand itself. As a former Polo Ralph Lauren regional manager explained in a 2018 interview, in response to their new customer demographic, the brand began manufacturing clothing based on what was popular with boosters. While Black people were excluded from Polo's formal aesthetic vision, they still swung the pendulum of what the brand produced and sold. While the Lo Lifes and their peers wore the same pieces as Polo's more high-end customers, their stylistic choices created an aesthetic that had nothing in common with the ads being shown on television. Their Polo shirts were accompanied by snapbacks, worn untucked over jeans, adorned with heavy gold chains. Polo continued to create staid and preppy marketing campaigns, but in the streets, the brand's clothing was becoming associated with a different kind of playfulness and panache.

In an interview with actor Michael K. Williams for the

Vice docuseries *Black Market*, one of the former Lo Life gang members told Williams, "We never did no gang shit, we was capitalists. How you gone call me a gang member when I got too much talent?" This quote highlights many of the tensions inherent in Polo boosting culture. For that former Lo Life member, doing "gang shit" means being illegitimate, a social pariah. It means fulfilling the stereotype of what a young, poor Black man in Brooklyn in the 1980s might be doing with his time. Being a capitalist means you're still engaging in violence, just in a way that's rewarded by mainstream society. In many ways, the allure and promise of Polo boosting was mobility from gang shit to capitalist shit. Founded by a working-class Jewish man who grew up in the Bronx, the Ralph Lauren brand was simultaneously exclusive and democratic, selling a vision of wealth and luxury that could be "yours for just twenty dollars." In interviews about Polo boosting, Lo Life members have repeatedly stated that people could get killed for their Polo. The violence of people stabbing and shooting one another to get Polo clothes is a surreal underside of the shiny, staid fantasy sold by Polo Ralph Lauren.

As Polo grew in popularity among young Black and Latino people, the brand became a mainstay of hip-hop fashion. One of the most famous instances of Polo in hip-hop culture is the 1994 music video for the Wu-Tang Clan's "Can It Be All So Simple." In the video, Raekwon wears a yellow and red Polo pullover with the words "Snow Beach" emblazoned across the front. The pullover came from a 1993 collection inspired by technical snowboarding wear. After the "Can It Be All So Simple" video was released, the piece became an iconic collector's item. Reflecting on the moment in an interview with Lo Life founder Thirstin Howl, Raekwon said, "I was definitely inspired by Lo Lifes because they were a bunch of wild assassin young niggas." In 2018, Polo re-released the Snow Beach collection, a move that many saw as an embrace of the brand's hip-hop history.

In more recent years, rapper Kanye West has become perhaps the most well-known figure to center Polo in his personal style. In 2013, a clip began circulating of West in an interview with radio host Sway, saying, "It ain't no Ralph though." That line, which rapidly became a meme, came from a conversation about business practices. Sway attempted to give West advice about his ventures, referencing his own experience creating a clothing line—the name of which we still don't know, as it may or may not exist. West repeatedly interrupted him, implying Sway's business wasn't on the same level with the grand, vaguely outlined vision West was trying to achieve.

West's obsession with Polo has been well-documented. In the early 2000s, he was often photographed in pastel Polo shirts. His 2004 music video for "All Falls Down" features West in a light pink polo with a mustard stain at the bottom—both a cheeky disruption and a mischievous form of worship. That same year, he appeared on MTV's *Total Request Live* wearing an orange and blue striped polo with a gold chain, a look that was re-created by his daughter North in a 2023 TikTok video. These are just two of many Kanye ensembles that have included Polo shirts. In 2015, photos surfaced of West at New York Fashion Week looking thrilled to finally meet Ralph Lauren in person. However, while West may idolize Polo and its aesthetics, his relationship with the brand is complicated. In a 2005 song "Diamonds from Sierra Leone," he gestures to the complexities of consumerism, saying, "Spend your whole life trying to get that ice. On a Polo rugby, it look so nice. How can something so wrong make me feel so right?"

Despite being one of Polo's most famous fans, West has always been self-conscious about how wearing the brand affects his image. Although his Polo outfits have often aligned with traditional hip-hop fashions, West has also gestured toward Polo's promise of shape-shifting, a way of accessing white America's iconic brand and using it for his own gain. In his 2010 song "Gorgeous," West raps, "As long as I'm in Polo smiling, they think they got me. But they would try to crack me if they ever saw a Black me." "Gorgeous" is from the album *My Beautiful Dark Twisted Fantasy*, a project West later described as a backhanded apology for his outburst at the 2009 MTV Video Music Awards. He has said that while 80 percent of the album's sentiments were genuine, the remainder of the album was created to "fulfill a perception" for the public. This album was followed by *YEEZUS* in 2013. In the *YEEZUS* song "New Slaves," West mocks Black people's engagement with mainstream fashion, arguing that their materialism—their gullibility to being seduced by fur coats and Alexander Wang—keeps them in bondage. In some ways, *My Beautiful Dark Twisted Fantasy* can be read as West's last appeal to establishment culture, and to the promise of legibility that Polo may have offered.

*　　*　　*

In 1764, an enslaved Black child named Julius Soubise arrived in London from Jamaica. He became the personal servant and close companion to the Duchess of Queensberry, who freed him from slavery and gave him the education a young, white member of the nobility would receive. Trained in horseback riding and fencing, Soubise soon became known as an exceptional horseman. He was eventually hired as a lead riding instructor by the acclaimed fencer and equestrian Domenico Angelo. Soubise was seen as an exotic attraction to those around him, doted on by the wealthy white women in the duchess's circle. When Soubise entered his late teens and early twenties, he embraced an extravagant lifestyle and aesthetic language, spending large amounts of money on carefully curated clothing. As Edward Scobie quotes in *Black*

Britannia: A History of Blacks in Britain, one observer described Soubise wearing a "powdered wig, white silk breeches, very tight coat and vest . . . enormous white neck cloth, white silk stockings, diamond-buckled red-heeled shoes." Soubise was known as a fop, a macaroni—a young man-about-town who frequented social clubs and the opera, disposed to preening, often dressing in clothing that was seen as gaudy or feminized by more conservative sectors of society. When Soubise embraced this polarizing and demanding aesthetic, it endangered his position as the doted-on pet of the wealthy. Where before he was a docile and novel young man, an exception to the rules that generally governed Black entry into white society, he was now becoming hard to manage, over-the-top, and disobedient. He was ultimately sent away to Calcutta to "mend his wild ways from the high life of the rakes," with some speculating that he was leaving to cover up sexually violent behavior toward the duchess's maid. There he lived comfortably as the founder of a fencing and equestrian school.

Throughout his young adulthood, Soubise's relationship with horses acted both as a marker of wealth and social capital and as a source of financial mobility and survival. As Monica L. Miller writes in *Slaves to Fashion: Black Dandyism and the Styling of Black Diasporic Identity*, Soubise was not fully a member of the servant class or the leisure class, which meant he still had to find a profession. His training as an equestrian was one of the many forms of education that set him apart from slaves and commoners of all races. A well-liked riding instructor for the nobility, Soubise was able to gain connections and a degree of acceptance from those who held power over his social position and access to resources. And after his later fall from grace, his knowledge of fencing and equestrian sports provided a way for him to establish himself in a new place. In Calcutta, as elsewhere, horses were part of a practice of European colonial luxury and hierarchy. While the symbol and image of the horse would become an exported shorthand for affluence in later centuries, the actual skills and sport of riding were important in maintaining social order in colonial Europe. Knowledge of equestrian sports signified status, a status that was not easily ceded to outsiders. Among the duchess's friends, some held the sentiment that "it was all very well to give the little negro an occupation, but that fencing and riding were likely to arouse in him rather lofty expectations which might not be fulfilled."

In many respects, Soubise's embrace of macaroni style can be seen as a form of resistance against the strictures of his life. While he was celebrated and praised, Soubise was also a deeply isolated figure. Set apart from the "common" Black slaves and freedmen in London at the time, he carried the complex eroticism of both a foppish ladies' man and a sexual outcast from the wealthy white circles he frequented. By ostentatiously spending the duchess's money on clothes and finery, he flaunted his access to capital, exercising what power he did have within a colonial economy. However, like the Lo Lifes, his bold claims to a visual language of white wealth still existed within the confines of consumerism. From eighteenth-century London to twentieth-century New York, these were young people who held tenuous agency within consumer cultures built variously by the systems of plantation slavery, Global South labor exploitation, Reagan-era anti-Black oppression, and genocidal WASP fantasies of American life. Through boosting Polo Ralph Lauren, the Lo Lifes laid claim to a vision of ease and abundance that had systemically been denied them. Soubise, on the other hand, disrupted his role as a plaything for the wealthy by making lifestyle and fashion choices that challenged his perception as an object of the white nobility's anxieties and desires.

In *Slaves to Fashion: Black Dandyism and the Styling of Black Diasporic Identity*, Monica L. Miller chronicles the history of Black people who have created their own extravagant and theatrical reinterpretations of traditional European style on their own terms, forming entirely new visual vocabularies and identities in the process. With its history of aesthetic subversion and interplay with white upper-class styles, dandyism is a thread that runs through many kinds of Black sartorial life, including the stories of Soubise and the Lo Lifes.

However, making your own choices about what to buy and wear can't by itself liberate you from centuries-old systems of oppression. Discussing the political utility and role of such practices, Miller writes that "precisely because the primary tools of the dandy's art—clothing and dress—are tied to consumption, the ambiguity of the dandy's political power is amplified."

Influenced in many ways by the history of British clothing, dandy motifs often overlap with signifiers of equestrian chic: slim-cut tweed jackets, buttoned blazers, heeled leather boots, top hats, and jodhpurs. Dandy style can be seen on a host of contemporary figures whose styles dissemble and mock European bourgeois fashion while also claiming a distinctive African diasporic identity. These examples range from Harlem fashion designer Dapper Dan to rapper A$AP Rocky and Nigerian American singer Jidenna.

Jidenna is known for his three-piece suits, often incorporating flamboyantly bright colors, pants with cropped legs, bold socks, and West African fabrics. His outfits appear playful, he is elegantly coiffed, and he is almost self-consciously sleek. In a 2015 interview with *Fashion Bomb Daily*, he said his style influences include "the Harlem Renaissance with hints of traditional West African design." More standard fits within his industry, he noted, are casual street wear like snapbacks and jeans. "Although I am breaking the rules of hip-hop culture by wearing a suit, I'm not too cool to sweat in it," he said. "I'm more concerned with the fit than fitting in." Central to the dandy aesthetic is a prioritization of style over conformity, a willingness to embrace too-muchness. Dandies break the rules, often making visible the cultural tensions and migratory histories that have shaped them and their dress. By citing the Harlem Renaissance and his Nigerian heritage as influences, Jidenna engages in a kind of transatlantic time travel, marking the geographies that have made the textiles of his clothing and his life possible.

In Jidenna's video "Classic Man," the artist showcases a range of dandy styles, appearing in a succession of three-piece suits, and accessorized with hats and canes. As suggested by the title, the song is about someone who embodies a suave, retro form of masculinity, a ladies' man who is simultaneously sexually forward and unfailingly respectful ("I can be a bull while I'm being polite"). The video moves through a series of all-Black social spaces, including a speakeasy and a barbershop. In the barbershop, a man is sitting with a poster behind him that says "I AM A MAN" in red letters. The slogan and poster date back to the civil rights movement—during the Memphis sanitation worker strike in 1968, protestors carried these signs to declare their humanity. Jidenna's "classic man" is both impeccably dressed and socially conscious. He's friendly with the men and good with the ladies. In one scene, he wears a white suit jacket with a bright orange wax-cloth print lining the lapel. While Jidenna's styling is creative and fun to look at, his approach to fashion also exemplifies some of the contradictions inherent in dandyism. It's important not to overstate the boundary-breaking possibilities of fashion; a suit with wax cloth looks nice, but how deeply does it engage a conversation about Jidenna's heritage and family migration histories? Central to the idea of the dandy is an exaggeration and subversion of traditional European clothing motifs, but where is the line between creatively mimicking such fashions and simply reproducing them with a little twist? At what point do contemporary nods to dandyism, and to syncretized fashion histories, aestheticize colonial violence? Jidenna's "classic" style is shaped by a kind of bourgeois Afromodernism, a cosmopolitan sensibility that infuses West African motifs into Western dress forms to create a *vibe*, with no elaboration on the ineffable losses and forced migrations that brought these cultural forms together in the first place.

For oppressed people, fashion can provide many things—a source of community building, a site of joy, a place to ask questions about one's conditions and histories, a place of refusal—but it doesn't on its own constitute collective freedom. The story of Black people's use of equestrian-influenced fashions is one of economic ingenuity, world-building, and the complex relationships between consumerism, capital, and cultural extraction. It's important that we don't valorize these fashions as a solution, because we would miss how they ask questions, provide openings, and invite us into further action.

*   *   *

While descriptions of dandy culture have historically focused on men, women and nonbinary people have also reinterpreted the language of suits, top hats, and oxfords. In the Republic of the Congo, a group of women called the Sapeuses don linen suits, silk socks, and ties, bringing dapper style to their neighborhoods. The Sapeuses see themselves as doing an emotional service for their communities, lifting spirits through the creativity of their dress. In the United States, artists like Janelle Monáe have created personal styles that reference the sharply tailored dandy aesthetic. In the early stages of their career, Monáe became well-known for the signature black suits, crisp white shirts, and bow ties they would wear onstage. Monáe explained in an interview with *Access Hollywood* that their style was an homage to their working-class parents: "They wore uniforms and so I wore black and white as my own uniform to pay homage to them." Monáe's father was a truck driver, and their mother worked as a janitor. While their style plays with the aesthetics of the wealthy, Monáe's comments point to the ways in which dandyism (and specifically Black dandyism) is also rooted in working-class lives, in the lives of servants, low-wage workers, and the enslaved. Photographer Shantrelle Lewis writes that "the black dandy entered Western history when enslaved Africans were made to dress

up extravagantly in order to represent their owners. . . .
The luxuriously dressed servants became more than status
symbols when they personalized their uniforms with their
own sense of pride and style." In dandy dress, there is a
blurring of class signifiers, representing the various roles
that tailored suiting has played in signifying labor, power,
and servility.

I grew up in the era of *DapperQ*, a fashion blog celebrating masculine-leaning queer and lesbian style. In middle and
high school, my first online examples of queer women's fashion were the models on *DapperQ* and similar sites. They wore
snapbacks and crisp button-downs, bow ties and oxfords. As
I look back as an adult, my past admiration of these styles
sometimes makes me cringe. In retrospect, my first forays
into queer fashion feel so limited—so closely modeled on
white men's office wear, so intently focused on a twee and
gentlemanly form of dress, so insistent on just a few ways
to be hot, queer, and not a femme. When I think about this
time in my life, I feel saddened by the kinds of selves available to me, and that embracing a more masculine sense of
style also meant navigating a white (and white-collar) stylistic language. But I wonder if the framework of the dandy
might offer an opportunity to approach that cultural and
personal moment with more generosity. The clothes we
wear reflect the violence of colonialism and the aesthetic
losses and negotiations we're forced to confront. For centu-

ries, Black dandies have engaged with these negotiations in ways that are playful, polarizing, demanding, and inventive.

★   ★   ★

The images of the horse and the equestrian haunt this essay, but for the Black people I'm writing about, horses were either a faraway and inaccessible dream, or a precarious and fraught privilege—a slippery slope to becoming an uppity, "lofty" negro. When we're talking about fashion, most often we're talking about excess, about choices people make that aren't seen as necessary in the strictest sense of the word. In what can almost be read as a rejoinder to Kanye's argument in "New Slaves," the poet-scholar Fred Moten insists commodities are not "dirty," but rather, in their many forms, help to "structure our social life." Black people arrived in the New World as commodities to be bought, traded, and sold. "I'm the descendant of commodities," Moten says, "and bear the trace of that . . . in my own flesh," a history that makes him feel that he can't be moralistic about people's relationships to commodities. I don't think commodities are morally neutral—rather, I think it's important to be critical about the labor that produces our commodities and the processes that bring them to us. It matters if our commodities are people, and it matters if the commodities we rely on for survival have been made by exploited human hands. Commodities, and how we consume them, always carry a moral weight. Under capitalist racism, Black people may engage inventively with their role as consumers, but their own existences and creations remain items to be bought and sold.

The relationships between Black people, clothing, and the image of the horse—all commodities under plantation slavery and capitalism—have significantly shaped material culture, music, and the visual architectures of our world. These stories confirm style is never simply surface level— central to these aesthetic rebellions is a recurring motif of violence and theft. In the *Vice* documentary, Williams talks about how Polo has now integrated hip-hop culture into its contemporary image, capitalizing on its popularity with the Black community. He notes, "Fashion brands are stealing styles from the same people who stole their clothes." Dandies, Lo Lifes, Soubise and his fellow "exceptional" servants and livery slaves in colonial England—these groups have all taken a kind of pleasure in the joyful rewriting of styles and ways of being that were never meant for them. Whether their horses are on their television screens or in their stables or merely suggested through the cut and tailoring of their jackets, Black people reappropriated equestrian fashion in ways that have forever changed what it means to be "equestrian chic."

COWBOY CARTER

A barbecue competition, a youth science fair, and a mutton busting contest where children attempt to stay on the backs of sheep racing wildly around an arena: these are just a few of the events that take place at the annual Houston Livestock Show and Rodeo. Founded in 1932 as the Houston Fat Stock Show, the twenty-day-long extravaganza regularly draws crowds of over a million people. Most of the rodeo and music events are held in Houston's NRG Stadium. It was here, in 2004, that a twenty-two-year-old Beyoncé rode into the stadium on the back of a palomino horse. In videos of that day, she wears a sequined top and a flowing gold skirt, with delicate sandals tucked into bulky leather stirrups. Riding slowly around the stadium before her performance, she raises each hand and waves at the crowd like a pageant queen.

In the 1950s, regional cowboy associations started organizing trail rides to the Houston Fat Stock Show. Riders would gather and travel together, often riding several days until they reached Houston's Memorial Park, where they would spend the night. In 1957, rodeo rider and cowboy Myrtis Dightman organized the first Black trail riding contingent to travel to the show. When Dightman and his riders reached Memorial Park, they faced hostility from the white riders already camped out there. Eventually, armed guards had to escort them into the park.

Since the inception of rodeo culture in Texas in the late nineteenth century, the sport was dominated by white riders. Long before Dightman convened his trail ride to attend the Fat Stock Show, Black riders had been carving out rodeo spaces of their own. During the 1940s, a network of small-town Black rodeos emerged, known as the Soul Circuit. The Soul Circuit led to the creation of the Southwest Colored Cowboys Association, an organization that held "All-Colored" rodeos and counted Dightman among its members.

Growing up in Houston's Third Ward, Beyoncé was surrounded by the history of rodeos and Black cowboy culture. She attended the Houston Livestock Show and Rodeo annually with her family, before performing at the event repeatedly throughout the early 2000s. She later cited the Soul Circuit among the inspirations for her fashion line Ivy Park's rodeo-themed collection, which she hoped would pay homage to the Black riders who shaped rodeo culture in Texas.

In the decades following her 2004 performance at the rodeo, horses have appeared in many forms throughout Beyoncé's work. In the opening shot of the video for "Run the World (Girls)" released in 2011, she rides a black horse through a postapocalyptic desert landscape, her hair flowing as she passes the detritus of a world on fire—a trash can lit ablaze, crates and wooden boxes littering the ground. She wears an all-white outfit with cowboy fringes flowing from the shoulders of her shirt. At the end of the scene, her horse rears as she stares into the camera. The images of her on horseback segue into continued scenes of conflict: cops in riot gear, a lion, a bull, a Beyoncé-led army of women prepared for combat. Here, the horse evokes traditionally militaristic postures of power, elevating Beyoncé as she surveys a landscape of destruction, highlighting her courage and strength. In these scenes, the horse becomes part of a visual vocabulary of power, providing Beyoncé with the eagle-eyed position of a battle surveyor.

Elsewhere in Beyoncé's work, horses tell a more intimate and personal story. In the video for "Daddy Lessons," part of the 2016 album *Lemonade*, horses are portrayed as part of the small-town Southern landscape Beyoncé locates as a place of origin. Black people riding on horseback along a dusty road are shown as if through a car window. A young girl and her father (presumably representing Beyoncé and her father) ride together down a quiet residential street.

Images of a grown-up Beyoncé riding on horseback are collaged with actual home videos of her childhood self talking to her father. Here, horses are part of a Black South that is a place of roots and ancestry, nostalgia, a foundation myth. The horses in this video aren't rearing or charging into a fight. Instead, they are walking through a Black landscape that is at once mundane and layered with meaning. Here, a horse isn't a soldier preparing for battle or walking war-torn streets. A horse can be a friend, a way of getting around or getting to those you care about, a way of remembering love that has changed and become fraught with age. In 2011, Beyoncé fired her father, Matthew Knowles, from a position as her manager and became estranged from him. In the same year, her mother, Tina Lawson, finalized her divorce with Knowles, who had a history of infidelity in their marriage. In an album marked by the realities of men's unfaithfulness and misogyny, "Daddy Lessons" looks backward with both yearning and anger, recognizing the ways Beyoncé's father taught her to protect herself from men just like him.

It's worth noting that "Daddy Lessons" is also the song that became the center of a controversy at the 2016 Country Music Association Awards, where Beyoncé performed it along with the country band Dixie Chicks (now known as the Chicks). The performance generated backlash from white country music fans, who argued the song—and by extension, Beyoncé—was an impostor, that it didn't belong in the country genre to which the musician was laying claim. The roots of the genre are inextricable from Black musical traditions, from the West African–originated banjo to Black fiddle music to the spirituals, hymns, and folk songs that continue to be adapted and performed by country musicians. The compositional innovations of enslaved musicians helped create hillbilly music, which evolved into what we now know as country. Numerous white country stars, including Hank Williams and Johnny Cash, were mentored and taught by Black musicians who often remained unnamed and unacknowledged. Despite Black people's foundational role in country music, "Daddy Lessons" generated intense debate about what, and whose, sounds belonged at a place like the CMA Awards.

Three years later, there would be a similar controversy over Lil Nas X's "Old Town Road." Incorporating a banjo, a Nine Inch Nails sample, and a classic Roland TR-808 trap beat, "Old Town Road" is a country rap song that combines familiar country imagery—tractors, cowboy hats, rodeos—with Fendi sports bras, Maseratis, and Lil Nas X's trademark playfulness and flippancy. The song spent one week on Billboard's Hot Country Songs chart, before the magazine removed it and placed it on the Hot Rap Songs chart instead. In explanation, Billboard released a statement saying that the song "incorporates references to country and cowboy imagery [but] does not embrace enough elements of today's country music to chart in its current version." Country singer Billy Ray Cyrus was among those who spoke up in support of Lil Nas X, arguing that "Old Town Road" did belong in the genre of contemporary country music. The two artists made a remix of "Old Town Road" that was nominated for Musical Event of the Year at the CMA Awards, a decision many fans saw as a snub to a song that could have been nominated for Single of the Year.

The country music establishment's reaction to "Old Town Road" and "Daddy Lessons" treads well-worn paths: the refusal to acknowledge Black musicians' presence outside of hip-hop, the quibbling over the boundaries of genre, the hot and cold response from awards shows and publications. Both songs' enormous success with listeners begs the question: Does acceptance from Billboard or the CMA Awards really matter to how the music moves through the world? What I'm most interested in is how Beyoncé and other Black artists making country music have engaged with the horse as they deal with these tensions around categorization, belonging, and lineage.

In contrast to the nostalgic, camcorder-footage ambiance of the "Daddy Lessons" video, the video for the "Old Town Road" remix with Billy Ray Cyrus is a kooky, time-traveling adventure tale. It starts off in the style of a cowboy Western, with Lil Nas X as a hard-riding bandit being chased by three riders. The riders eventually give up the chase, with one saying, "When you see a Black man on a horse going that fast, you just gotta let him fly." Narrowly missing a bullet from a white homeowner, Lil Nas X runs into a tunnel that also happens to be a time portal. He and his horse come out the other side and emerge into 2019 on Old Town Road, a street running through a modern-day Black community. Lil Nas X rides down the road looking like a character from a dusty Western town in a historical drama, attracting disbelieving stares from the residents of the block. He ends up making friends, and his horse becomes a neighborhood attraction for the kids. Cut to Lil Nas X and Billy Ray Cyrus in full cowboy glam, sporting bedazzled fringed jackets and hats. They walk into a white folks' bingo night in an auditorium and start performing "Old Town Road" on the stage. Eventually, the bingo players start square dancing—they look like they're having a great time. The video is full of winks to Lil Nas X's outsider status in country music, from the run-in with the property owner to the shocked stares from the bingo players. The film's opening scenes gesture toward the novelty of seeing "a Black man on a horse," and his reception from the residents of Old Town Road communicates a different kind of singularity. While the main plotlines are resolved with moments of collective joy and celebration (the Old Town Road kid dancing on top of the horse, the enthusiastic bingo players tearing up the floor), there remains a persistent note of awkwardness and absurdity. Lil Nas X as an eighteenth-century Wild West bandit is fundamentally out of place in 2019, no matter how warmly he is welcomed. In the closing scenes, Lil Nas X and his backup performers take turns smiling awkwardly at the camera. He then poses with an older white lady, both of them sporting the nervous, plastic facial expressions of prom photo subjects.

Horse imagery is an intuitive feature of country music. While the "Daddy Lessons" video pictures Black riders and horses in a naturalistic setting, laying claim to the geographies of country music as a matter of course, "Old Town Road" uses the cowboy and his horse to poke at the concept of authenticity. In "Old Town Road," the horse is a shtick, a historical anomaly, a genre convention that is at once earnest and contrived. The "Old Town Road" video reminds us that no matter how deep your history with horses, no matter how true to genre your country music is, being a Black artist still means inhabiting a position of exclusion. It'll be awkward and weird, they'll question your credentials and stare as you enter the auditorium, but at the end of the night, you just might have the whole room on its feet anyway.

*   *   *

In 2022, Beyoncé released her seventh studio album, *Renaissance*. The album cover features the singer sitting astride a holographic horse. The disco-ball vibes are a fitting match for the album, which draws heavily from dance music genres like house and disco, paying homage to the queer artists who shaped these traditions. Fans named the horse Reneigh, and it became an expected prop at *Renaissance* tour performances.

During Beyoncé's *Renaissance* tour stop in Amsterdam, there was a malfunction with the disco horse she was sitting on. After telling the audience she wanted to do something different that night and "get closer" to them, she stayed on the horse while her crew seemed to experience some confusion. Beyoncé motioned to them to move the stairs that were next to her and the horse. The crew eventually helped her, but not before she sang the entirety of "Summer Renaissance." These moments were posted on YouTube by a fan, to the entertainment and chagrin of some commenters. Watching the video, I thought about the distance between fantasy and lived reality, between the glimmering two-dimensional photo of Beyoncé on the disco horse and the reality of being a performer relying on an unwieldy and imperfect prop during a concert. There is something about the image of the horse that can be larger than life, that can encourage us to blur the boundaries between our desires and the unglamorous truths, the hidden labors of the everyday. But being on a horse—or being on a horse-shaped prop during a stop on your international tour—is a tricky, vulnerable, and precarious thing.

Five months after the Amsterdam tour stop, Beyoncé screened the *Renaissance* film in Israel. At the time, Israel was two months into its attack on Palestine's Gaza Strip that had begun in October 2023. By early December, over seventeen thousand Palestinians had been killed. Despite widespread calls from her fans not to show the film in Israel because of the ongoing genocide, Beyoncé proceeded with the screening. The Israeli government posted to Beyoncé on X (formerly Twitter) with a video of an Israeli girl who had been taken hostage and then released by Hamas. "@Beyonce there's a little girl named Emily who's been through a lot and would love to meet you," the tweet read. The tweet included a video featuring Emily's dad, who talked about his commitment to bringing his daughter to a Beyoncé concert after she recovered. "I don't care where it is in the world; she's going," he said. It's notable that the state addressed Beyoncé directly through its X account, invoking her in a narrative about Israeli innocence and childhood purity through this video. There's no doubt many of the thousands of Palestinian children who had been murdered by Israel would have loved to see Beyoncé too.

Beyoncé is a multimillionaire pop star with an almost unthinkable amount of cultural influence, and every decision she makes is subject to intense debate. Is Beyoncé a Zionist? Does Beyoncé have a responsibility to make a statement about the genocide? Is Beyoncé endorsing war crimes?

The avatars of the elite are often subject to such collective anxieties, even when their alignments have long been made clear. As the writer Momtaza Mehri writes of Black people's relationships with the celebrities who are said to represent us, "Our pleasures are inflected with responsibility. Can we confront what they reveal?"

In the *Renaissance* film, the image of the disco horse ushers in a behind-the-scenes story of Beyoncé as diva, hardworking mother, and auteur. In the Tel Aviv movie theaters screening *Renaissance*, the glamour of the holographic horse contrasted sharply with the real horses surviving in Gaza less than a hundred miles away. Throughout the war on Gaza, horses have played a role in transporting wagons filled with refugees fleeing south. Stables that were home to long traditions of Palestinian horsemanship have been decimated along with homes, hospitals, universities, libraries, and countless cultural institutions. Even before the latest bombardment began in October 2023, Palestinian riders struggled to access space and resources for their horses. After Gaza's only airport was bombed by Israel in 2001, its ruins became the site of an annual horse race that drew attendees from throughout the Strip. Here, again, the pop music horse gestures to the gaps between fantasy and reality, between the image sold to eager fans and the devastating experiences of occupation. Whether we are fans cheering in a stadium or people relying on horses for transportation and survival, our relationships to horses both real and imagined are inextricably connected to our relationships with empire. Nowhere is this clearer than with the horses populating our music video and pop performance dreams.

*   *   *

Beyoncé's latest album, *Cowboy Carter*, was released in the spring of 2024. On the album cover, Beyoncé rides backward on a white horse, wearing a long-sleeved shirt and chaps in red, white, and blue. She holds the American flag in one hand, its stripes visible in the corner of the image. The cover reliably ignited controversy, with its bold Americana leading to a variety of interpretations, from gauche nationalism to satire to a paean to Black rodeo culture. Unlike Reneigh, the *Cowboy Carter* cover horse is a living, breathing being. Perhaps this shift from disco ball to flesh indicates a realism demanded by more somber times: It's a particularly fraught election year, Beyoncé has turned her focus to questions of nation and legacy, and who has time for the club in this economy?

Throughout *Cowboy Carter*, the horse is an accessory to the various personas Beyoncé assumes, from the lovers hitting the road in "Sweet Honey Buckiin'" to the brooding, peripatetic figure in "Just for Fun" who hides his identity from the cowboys and the "rodeo circus." The album brings together collaborators like Dolly Parton, Willie Nelson, and Black country star Linda Martell, along with lesser-known artists like country rap musician Shaboozey, for a wide-ranging work that explores the boundaries of genre and reimagines familiar tropes of country music. Of course, Beyoncé's collaborators include her audience members too. I came to know *Cowboy Carter* not only through an isolated listening experience, but also through the Tik-Toks and Reels shot by Black riders and set to its tracks, the digital content of Black Southerners who provided context and meaning for the album's many references. The horses of *Cowboy Carter* are numerous; they are the trail horses carrying their riders to a zydeco dance in Louisiana, the ponies led by young Black girls on a family farm, the horses ridden by urban cowboys through the busy streets of Austin. It is partly through these horses and their riders that the album lives and moves through the world, becoming a soundtrack to the artistry and joy of Black Southern riders.

Cowboy Carter begins with the song "American Requiem," which combines the beginnings of a rallying cry ("Can we stand for something?") with references to Beyoncé's exclusion from the very American establishment of country music ("Then the rejection came, said I wasn't country 'nough"). The last track is "Amen," a gospel-influenced song saturated with the imagery of failed national myths. These two tracks bookend an album in which the critique promised by the title "American Requiem" is often approached, then backed away from. In "Ya Ya," a song that points to the debt and chronically low wages endemic to working-class life, Beyoncé asks, "You looking for a new America?" It's a question the album never elaborates on.

In "Some Notes on Song," John Berger writes that "songs refer to aftermaths and returns, welcomes and farewells. Or to put it another way: songs are sung to an absence." *You looking for a new America?* It is this enduring absence, this unspoken yearning, that runs through the heart of *Cowboy Carter.* As figures that illuminate Beyoncé's relationship to genre, power, and nation, the horses of her oeuvre have come to represent the grief and violence at the heart of the American Dream. In mirrored disco-ball silver or in flesh, on dirt roads or on movie theater screens, Beyoncé's horses trouble the easy conclusions we are sold, urging us to ask what, exactly, we are looking for.

WHEN NO SOFTNESS CAME

In Diedrick Brackens's tapestry *when no softness came*, a child rides a horse backward, leaning against its mane and dangling their limbs down the horse's side. The child is woven in bright green yarn, highlighted starkly against the white of the horse. The horse seems to be in a rush. The child has given in to stillness.

When no softness came, we looked for the tired in each other's knees. Held it up by our fingertips, wove a bed where we might dream. When no softness came, I cried in the shower and gave my anger to the sea. I forgot I wasn't alone until the spirit with 916 selves came and goaded me into staying alive. Reclining backward on a moving horse, the figure in the tapestry looks like they're doing an impossible thing. I recognized it as I walked through the gallery, the taut and tender of seeking rest in a place swirling with its impossibility.

The Black cowboys they show us in school, in movies

and magazine articles are upright, stoic. They look out at us defiantly from grayscale photographs, demanding we mark their presence in the expansionist and messy histories of the so-called American West. Growing up, I never thought to ask if Bass Reeves was sometimes tired after long days chasing horse thieves and wrangling cattle on Chickasaw land. If Stagecoach Mary ever just wanted to lie next to the woman she traveled over a thousand miles for and never deliver mail again. The image of the horse—in visual art, in archives—sometimes seems irretrievably bound up with a mythos of masculinity and war, the imperative of action. The back of a horse is so often the site for the most scripted discursive struggles about *who we can be.*

In his book *The Sovereignty of Quiet,* Kevin Quashie writes that Black culture is often reductively identified with an idea of loud public resistance. The Olympians with their fists in the air, the Black Lives Matter protesters, the civil rights protesters, the teenagers marching for safety they shouldn't have to demand. Quashie writes that this unrelenting insistence on Black publicness makes it easy to overlook the complex power of our quiet and vulnerable moments. I think this is why I love images of Black people doing the everyday, freed from the responsibility to produce collective absolvement and inspiration. When I saw *when no softness came,* something in my body lay down in relief, stretched and unfurled into an imagined otherwise. There were no grand proclamations here, no rigid spines. The figure in the tapestry could be gathering their energy for battle or racing their friends to the lake, but they are under no obligation to tell us which. Secrets are allowed here. My Black interior is allowed here. In the infinite space before the horse's hooves meet the ground, our stubborn and inconsistent inner selves are tended to, given the queer gift of new shapes for the body, new imaginations of posture, lessons whispered in a world that never lets us stop moving.

For Quashie, "quiet . . . is a metaphor for the full range of one's inner life." It isn't quite the same as being motionless or silent, although it can include those things. Rather, it's a way of thinking about all the moments when we are not being conscripted into notions of public representation. It's lingering over the food you're preparing in the morning, tending your windowsill plants after work and before the kids need dinner, close-reading screenshots with the group chat for no purpose greater than a laugh and the insistent, wordless love you have for your friends. It's settling down to do nothing in particular after you've washed the outside off. When I think about this concept of quiet, my first impulse is to berate myself for not having fully achieved it, for always feeling like I have to be doing something, for overanalyzing my relationships, my actions, my play. Which is funny, considering Quashie's whole thing is that quiet is inherent to Black people, a birthright and an undefinable essence we carry inside us. We can try to run and perform all we like, but the quiet is still there, just by virtue of us being alive. Quashie suggests that a synonym for this quiet is "surrender," a practice often described as passive and undesirable. The deliberate action of yielding to the unknown.

*　　*　　*

As a child, I had trouble with the unknown, particularly that of overhead lights off and shadows on the walls, the hazy bedtime hours. I understood that one was supposed to drift gently to sleep, but drifting seemed too dangerous a surrender. Instead, I would stay up reading books illuminated by cheap plastic flashlights or the adjacent rooms where my mom was also awake, writing or talking on the phone to her friends until two or three in the morning. During those late nights, I would reread obsessively, hoping to quiet my brain and its never-ending loops and glitches with the mundane hum of words my eyes had scanned hundreds of times before. I would journal in spiral-bound notebooks where my angriest thoughts scrawled across the pages in huge cursive font, broadcasting a bigness and loudness I couldn't imagine embodying in the shame-filled daylight hours. I would sit by our desktop computer scrolling through my dad's sprawling library of music, playing Tracy Chapman or Bob Dylan on repeat in my headphones, a lone figure sitting in a small bubble of digitally generated light. I was always tired during the day. Always sitting on floors, slouching into corners, looking for excuses to lay my body down.

Growing up, my mom would play Mercedes Sosa cassettes on the stereo in our living room. Sunday mornings with the lights streaming through the blinds, singing along to "Duerme, Negrito." "Duerme, Negrito" is a Colombian and Venezuelan folk song about a mother who goes to work in the fields to provide for her son, the *negrito*. In the song, someone else is singing the child to sleep, telling him of his mother's labor and her sadnesses (she works but they don't pay her, she works in mourning clothes, she works while she's sick and she's coughing). The narrator tells the little Black child his mother will bring back things for him from the field, that she'll return bearing pork and quail and fruit. She does this for you, the narrator tells the child. "Pal negrito chiquitito." For her small Black child.

I understood only the refrain of the song, which was also the part my mother would sing along to. I thought of it as a sad, slightly maudlin melody that was pretty but told me nothing new. I already knew Black people worked too hard. I was already struggling to sleep, already navigating a bundle of confused obligations and inherited grief. I was learning the language of debt to one's parents and assigned family, a vocabulary that could be at times deeply loving or sharply accusatory, a situation that felt as looped and inescapable as my nighttime thoughts. *She goes to work in her mourning clothes. She does this all for you.* It wasn't until I was an adult that I realized the song also contained a threat, that the rhythmic middle section I enjoyed was in fact a set of cautionary lyrics. After regaling the boy with names of the delicious food his mother will bring back, the narrator changes approaches. They warn that if the little Black child doesn't sleep, the white devil will come and eat his leg.

Mercedes Sosa was not herself Black, having been born of mestizo parents in a provincial capital of Argentina. Throughout her career, she was celebrated for her opposition to right-wing leaders and her dedication to the progressive, folk-inspired nuevo cancionero movement. In photos, she is often looking moodily off camera or gesturing mid-song, her shiny hair framing a peach-pale face. She was considered dark by the standards of a country that had systematically "diluted" its Black and Indigenous populations in the eighteenth and nineteenth centuries, a country whose president once claimed that "in Argentina Blacks do not exist; that is a Brazilian problem." And so she was called *la negra*. She was also called the voice of the voiceless, a nickname I can't help but find a little disappointing in its triteness.

In a 1976 video, Sosa sings "Duerme, Negrito" while holding a bombo legüero drum. It is easy to see why her performances made her known as an iconic interpreter of traditional songs. Her voice is silky, commanding, and luxurious. She caresses the words, sometimes smiling slightly on the refrain of "negrito." Every now and then, she punctuates her guitar-playing accompanist with light taps of the drum. The bombo legüero (not to be confused with the Puerto Rican bomba drum) was created by Spanish settlers in Argentina, modeled after the Indigenous instruments they encountered. A colonizer's drum that became a folk music staple. So often when songs of Black labor and struggle get popularized, the music becomes infinitely reproduced without context, even the performance of it shaped by our bodily absence, how they turn our pain and exhaustion into something romantic, picturesque, how they call us voiceless when what they really want is to hear themselves speak.

I'm thinking about how so many of the folk songs I grew up on, most of them sung by colonized people in various parts of the world, are just deeply tired. How so many of them speak of exhaustion, of working past the capacity of your body, how they are maps of the coping mechanisms we use to stay awake and alive. How these songs transform the backbreaking mundane into something worth making music about, something we might dance together to in the kitchen at the end of a long day, something a child might sing the words to without realizing the weight of the story being told. How they call us into collective resistance of a world that demands our unending labor, how they mark the scarce and temporary cessations of work as events worth celebrating. A soundtrack to our quiet. "Work all night on a drink of rum!" I would sing along gleefully with Harry Belafonte's recording of the Jamaican song "Day-O." "Stack banana till the morning come, daylight come and me wan' go home."

For all of Sosa's exhortations toward an unencumbered sleep, I still found myself as a child unable to let go of the tense alertness, the hunched vigilance I carried with me everywhere like a loaded gun. In my refusal to sleep, I could create a different world for a few hours at a time. A world where I touched the furniture like a lover, feeling for the journals and pens I had stashed the night before. A world where I touched myself as if laying claim to my skin, re-learning the fiction that, despite all my experience living, I still wanted so badly to believe—that my body was my own.

That's why, when I saw the figure in the tapestry, I smiled to myself. Kinfolk is t-i-r-e-d, and they ain't afraid to show it. They sleep? They dreaming? Maybe only in dreamspace could a little Black child gallop through the world backward, belly up and out, shoulders in sweet repose. From dream-space to gallery space, a spell that transmutes the matter of this reality. An incantation of *what could be*.

*   *   *

I've been thinking lately about some lines from Alexis Pauline Gumbs's collection *Dub*. "yes. i slept like a whale. one part of my brain always alert to drowning. . . . yes. i slept like the shipwrecked granddaughter i was. . . . so no. i never really slept." In *Dub*, Gumbs channels the voices of her Anguillan, Indigenous, and Irish ancestors. She writes as the beleaguered women, the overwhelmed mothers, the abandoning and abandoned men, the migrants and seers and spirits who make up her lineage. Sometimes constant alertness is a loaded gun handed to you by your forebears, passing on the exhaustion that kept them safe. Sometimes you're a shipwrecked granddaughter with hypervigilance grafted onto your bones.

In March 2022, I woke up from top surgery not breathing, an oxygen monitor beeping wildly behind me. Even when I tried to inhale consistently, I would stop breathing a little each time I fell back to sleep. Several months later, I tried to fall asleep in a hotel bed with wires strapped to my head and each of my limbs. In another room, a technician was measuring the quality of my rest, the length of my breaths, the number of times I jolted awake gasping for air. A quick online search had shown me that a predisposition toward sleep apnea could be inherited. Reading this, I remembered all the times my dad would fall asleep on the couch and wake up chasing his own breath, the times his chest would stop moving for several seconds and I would watch until it began again. I also learned that sleep disorders were linked to childhood trauma—I remembered all the times I stayed awake watching shadows on the ceiling, holding myself close, waiting for the footsteps or the crisis. It wasn't until I saw the child in Brackens's tapestry that I realized I wanted someone to carry me, to tell me I could rest now. Someone to tell me I could lay with my belly up and not be afraid, they'd sit at the edge of the bed and stay awake so I didn't have to. But shipwrecked granddaughters don't know if anyone will be alive to carry them. We learn to lie in wait, ready to spring into uprightness at a moment's notice. One part of our brains always alert to drowning.

During my years of horseback riding instruction, I was made intimate with a doctrine of uprightness. The body was supposed to be supple and responsive; one's lower back was to move organically with the rhythms of the horse's gait. But always, shoulders back. Eyes up. No slumping. Phrases repeated by many teachers—the husky-voiced Long Island women who spent their days carting kids to local horse shows, dry-cleaning outfits and loaning clothes when parents were too busy. The university coach who, after registering me and a Thai teammate for an event, joked that she missed the old days when people's last names were easier to spell. But always, shoulders back. I mean, and I'm sure you know, these institutions shape our frames. They have a vested interest in a stoic (Black) back. They have charts and things of how a body should be.

Another thing about uprightness: The first occurrences of horseback riding as sport in the Western world were linked to the military. In ancient Greece, equestrian games were established to build skills for combat. Throughout the history of the British Empire, practices and treatises of horsemanship were created with the mounted soldier at their center. I wonder what it means for me to shape my body inside a lineage of men's conquest, inside a received tradition of mastery over land and gender. To shape this scoliosis backbone, this Black and shipwrecked self, this mad. This exhausted. To mimic the postures of invading soldiers, because therein lies a kind of safety, or at least that's what we're told. Upright means productive, ready to kill.

*   *   *

I recently reread Ntozake Shange's *Sassafrass, Cypress & Indigo*, a novel about three Black sisters growing up in a family of South Carolina weavers. Their mother and the women before her have woven garments for the same white family since slavery, and now do so for money. The eldest daughter, Sassafrass, starts making artistic wall tapestries in high school, an impractical form of weaving that confuses her mother. Later, when Sassafrass weaves in front of her militant race man boyfriend, he chastises her for not doing something to uplift the Black condition. Sassafrass has visions while she weaves. She communes with spirits and finds moments of escape from her abusive household ("because when women make cloth, they have time to think"). In the tactile work of weaving, she shapes and remakes the material of her world. Refusing the gaze of her family's white employers, she makes a space of quiet, determined by the topographies and desires of her interior world.

In Brackens's weaving, an embodied practice that calls back to crucial and undervalued Black handcraft traditions, he reconfigures the possible. He gives us time to think, spaces to linger, moments to turn away from the demands of an unforgiving public and toward one another instead. When I stopped in front of the tapestry, and left and came back again, I felt the gift of it in my bones. When I look for lineage within the long canon of figures on horseback, the centuries of generals' statues and oil paintings, I choose this child woven of bright green yarn. Reclining on their way to who-knows-where, beckoning, *Listen, this is how a body can be.* Their horse with the unfinished tail and hanging threads, a haptic and imperfect vision of care.

Something I return to each time I look at this piece is the gentle echo between the human figure and the horse. The curve of the child's back mimicking the horse's neck and back, the call-and-response between the horse's legs and the child's dangling limbs. I think I'm learning that it's okay to surrender to what carries you. It's okay to be transported, to be tired and trustful in the presence of another. Witnessing the horse's movement and the child's gentle stillness and the frayed and knotted edges of the land they move across, I take hold of my younger self and lay my body down next to them. Maybe here is the quiet, a way out of the wreck.

Diedrick Brackens, *when no softness came*, 2019, cotton twine and threads, acrylic yarns, polyester thread (possible), dyes, 98½ × 101½ in. (250.2 × 257.8 cm).

AFTER THE CAMERAS

In the news photo on my screen, a young Black woman sits on the back of a brown horse in the middle of a city street. The rider and the horse helm a crowd of people lifting fists and protest signs above their heads, many of them wearing masks and bandannas over their faces. To the right of the horse, a protester carries a yellow sign that reads "We're tired of injustice." The rider wears blue jeans and has shoulder-length locks. She looks directly into the camera as she and her horse walk forward.

The rider in the photo is Brianna Noble, and in 2020, she famously attended a Black Lives Matter protest in Oakland with her horse Dapper Dan. In an interview with KQED, Noble said, "I decided to take my horse out to the protest to kind of change the narrative of what's going on. . . . A good, bright, positive image to focus on, as opposed to some of the destruction." She described Dapper Dan as the "partner that has my back."

That summer, the United States had erupted in protest after the murder of George Floyd, a forty-six-year-old Black man in Minneapolis who died after a white police officer knelt on his neck for almost ten minutes. Two months before Floyd was murdered, a Black woman named Breonna Taylor was killed in her home by police officers who broke into her apartment while she was asleep. One month before Breonna Taylor was killed, a Black man named Ahmaud Arbery was jogging in his neighborhood when he was killed by a white neighbor who assumed he was a burglar running from a crime scene.* In March, the country had gone into lockdown because of the COVID-19 pandemic. White-collar workers who could sign in remotely from the relative safety of their homes began doing so, while garbage collectors, delivery people, supermarket workers, warehouse

---

* In a previous draft of this manuscript, I named George Floyd, Ahmaud Arbery, and Breonna Taylor as Black people who were murdered by the police. During a call with the HarperCollins legal department, I was told that unless a judge had found the police guilty of murder, I would need to change my phrasing and instead use words like "killed" and "killing." To no one's surprise, the findings in cases of police brutality are a primer on the racism and injustice inherent to the American criminal justice system. For example, in August 2024, a federal judge ruled that Breonna Taylor's boyfriend, who shot at the police, was ultimately responsible for her death, although she was killed by police bullets. Later in the year, one of the Louisville Metro Police Department officers who fired blind shots into Taylor's home was found guilty of violating her constitutional rights. While legal distinctions are significant, terms like "excessive force" and "civil rights violations" can also serve to obscure the truth, creating a linguistic veil around the countless instances where Black people have been murdered by police officers and self-deputized white people.

workers, restaurant staff, and other low-wage essential workers risked their lives each day to ensure the continued functioning of an economy built on their labor. It was a season of death, a season of riots, when people spilled out into the streets to demand a different calculus for the living. And with them: the horses.

Black riders were a steady presence at Black Lives Matter protests across the country. Groups of riders from organizations like the Nonstop Riders in Houston and the Compton Cowboys in Los Angeles filled the streets along with marchers on foot, as did individual riders like Noble and "Dreadhead Cowboy" Adam Hollingsworth. The riders came to the protests with various aims—showing solidarity, lifting spirits, and debunking misinformation and fearmongering about the state of their neighborhoods. In doing so, they joined a lineage of riders throughout the Americas whose horses have accompanied them to protest against colonial violence, against gentrification and police brutality, against encroachments on their lives and neighborhoods. In 2016 and 2017, during demonstrations against the construction of the Dakota Access Pipeline, Indigenous horse riders were an integral part of the protesters' encampment at the Standing Rock Reservation. Riders formed safety patrols, scouting for signs of police and private security activity, and rode hundreds of miles along the pipeline. In 2023, residents of California's San Gabriel Valley formed a *cabalgata*—a mounted procession—to protest against proposed rezonings and development in their area, policies they said would destroy their long-standing traditions of backyard stables and neighborhood riding. In the *Los Angeles Times*, Mariana Duran wrote, "The mainly Latino and Latina riders from across the San Gabriel Valley wore traditional Mexican boots and gear. . . . Some made their horses dance to banda music played by musicians sitting in the back of a pickup truck that slowly wove between the procession."

In 2020, the horses in the streets were witness to collective grief and rage. With their riders, they were collaborators in expressing calls for a different world, practitioners of Black creativity amid the death and grief wrought by white supremacy. I remember coming home from a protest past the nighttime curfew, walking past the white cops gathered around the train station exit, taking the steps to my apartment two at a time and opening the door and lying on the couch and looking at my phone to see images of Black riders at protests in Houston, Oakland, Minneapolis. Even across time and space, their presence felt comforting and protective. Able to survey the crowd from their vantage point in the saddle, seated on large animals that could gallop the length of a city block at a moment's notice but were calm enough to walk in crowds full of screaming people, the riders were a reminder of the strength and power held by the collective. Together with their horses, they were an assurance of the webs of kinship that covered our bodies like a prayer, the ecological entanglements that were present even in the middle of an urban protest surrounded by traffic and concrete buildings.

The existence of Black protesters and their horses at Black Lives Matter demonstrations was a sharp counterpoint to the presence of another group of people on horseback—mounted cops. Police on horseback also exuded a feeling of power, but theirs was the power of the state, the power to arrest and kill, the ever-present threat of bodily harm against the people in the streets. There's a long history of mounted cops and state officials brutally attacking Black people. In 2019, a mounted officer in Galveston, Texas, led a handcuffed Black man named Donald Neely through the streets with a rope. At a demonstration in the summer of 2020, a Houston Police Department mounted officer trampled a protester in downtown Houston. In 2021, photographer Paul Ratje documented mounted Border Patrol agents chasing and whipping Haitian migrants near the US-Mexico border. Here, the horses' size, speed, and competence in crowds were weaponized—used as a way to enforce the borders of white "safety," private property, and the nation itself. As Atlanta-based activist Christopher "Soul" Eubanks said in an interview with *Sentient Media*, mounted police officers at protests were "another reminder of the violent origins of this country. . . . Police not only have the law on their side, the benefit of the doubt, and handheld weapons, but they also have the ability to use the body of another being to intensify their dominance." Like the horses used by slave patrols to pursue Black people who ran from the plantation, police horses are used as tools of surveillance and punishment, living bodies enlisted into the project of white supremacy.

In the months following George Floyd's murder, activists turned their attention not only to the living arbiters of racial violence but also to the monuments glorifying the histories of that violence. In 2020, at least ninety monuments of Confederate leaders were removed, some forcibly toppled by crowds of protesters and others removed by local governments eager to recuperate their image in the face of public scrutiny. The white men memorialized in these statues were generals and landowners who upheld the institution of slavery and the economies that it built. And in accordance with such traditions and the language of power they demanded, the statues of these men often portrayed them on horseback. From the John Breckinridge Castleman statue in Louisville to the statues of Stonewall Jackson in Lexington and Robert E. Lee in Richmond, these figures were elevated above passersby not only by stone pedestals but also by the horses on which they sat. For wealthy white men of the Confederacy, the saddle was a kind of throne, a symbol of ownership, a location from which to decree who lived and died. In their demands to remove the monuments, the protesters called for a revision of public memory, a dethroning.

Videos and photographs of the deaths of George Floyd and countless other Black people killed by police have been shared and viewed online millions of times. While some see this visual documentation as an important form of evidence, it can also fuel a gruesome cycle of voyeurism. As these images are circulated, a person becomes reduced to their last words, the anguish of their violent death, a Black person becoming a *Black body* in the endless discourse factory of the internet. George Floyd and Ahmaud Arbery were killed for the crime of being Black in public. One could argue that their Blackness was more celebrated in death than in life. In death, their images became arguments for the deservingness of Black people to live in safety, to grow old, to go for a run or buy a pack of cigarettes and come out the other side alive. Their names became metonyms for the foundational violences of America.

Endlessly circulated and reproduced in digital form, the visual languages of protest movements can easily become decontextualized, reduced from their original meaning into empty symbols. As Vincent Bevins writes in *If We Burn: The Mass Protest Decade and the Missing Revolution*, the contemporary focus on forms of protest like the street rally and demonstration emerged alongside the development of mass media in the 1950s and '60s. These forms of action were meant to grab radio and television coverage, creating spectacles and disruptions that threatened the authority of people in power. However, the relationship between media, visibility, and political change proved to be more complex than it may have seemed to organizers at the time. Like many popular movements, the Black Lives Matter movement saw its aesthetics and demands become co-opted by a white, liberal mainstream. Somehow, the movement's calls for a complete dismantling of the prison system became translated into members of Congress kneeling on the floor in kente cloth stoles, or your slightly racist co-worker posting a black square on her Instagram page, or a Black Lives Matter sign on a redlined suburban lawn. In the years following these gestures of supposed goodwill, there was a bipartisan backlash against the uprisings. While officials in many cities had initially committed to defunding police departments in some form, spending on police budgets actually increased between 2020 and 2022. One survey of more than one hundred cities and counties found that 83 percent were spending more on police in 2022 than they had three years prior.

When I remember the optimism and energy of the 2020 protests, I think, too, about the complicated, messy, and often invisible long haul of political struggle. I think about the organizers who spent their lives articulating the connections between capitalism and policing before the phrase "prison abolition" was ever mentioned in a major newspaper, and about those who stay and fight long after the last cameras have left.

Many people learned about Black urban cowboys for the first time while attending or watching footage of the protests. The riders they saw often hailed from local stables and horsemen's associations that had been doing community work for decades. These organizations are spaces for Black people to gather, to celebrate milestones like birthdays and graduations, to mourn instances of violence in their neighborhoods, to pass down knowledge about riding and animal care, to watch one another grow up. In Philadelphia, where I live, the members of the Fletcher Street Urban Riding Club (FSURC) have collectively raised generations of Black riders. The club was founded by Ellis Ferrell Jr. in 2004, but Black riders have owned stables on Fletcher Street for over a century. FSURC is both a keeper of Black cowboy history and a vibrant community hub. Among other initiatives, the club organizes trips to bring young riders to local farms and rodeos, offers pony rides at outdoor markets and street festivals, has summer and after-school programs, and collaborates on public art and documentary projects. Despite limited funding and the threats of increasing gentrification and development, the club has managed to sustain this space of education and ecological tending in its North Philly neighborhood. This, too, is work that resists the state-sanctioned violence against Black communities and supports the necessities of collective nourishment and survival, creating a place where histories of Black urban riding can be preserved and shared.

To live according to the dominant rules of our world requires a commitment to forgetting such histories. Every day, we are encouraged to forget the potential of our collective political power and to believe the best we can hope for is a return to an increasingly unlivable sense of "normalcy." We are told to forget genocides, pandemics, and the myriad ways that capitalism keeps us alienated and unwell. In their connection to histories of Black escape, organizing, rest, study, and protest, horses embody a refusal to forget. In an age of the flat and contextless viral image, the horse demands historicization; its presence raises questions about labor, geography, and relation, reminding us of the bloodshed and the care that brought us here, to this place and time. To look for the horse in the archives of our bodies, in the stories of those who came before us, in the words and images we use to understand our lives, is to insist on a simple but crucial question: What and who must we remember?

When I visit Fletcher on a Saturday morning, there are children bathing a dog on the sidewalk, painting a fence and arguing over who gets to hold the brush, looking for chicken eggs behind the horse stalls, chasing down a cat, and carrying old saddles out of the shed. They show me the Angora rabbits with impossibly long winter coats and give me advice on how to approach the most skittish horses. And as I have for most of my life and for lifetimes before this, I will place my hand on a horse's shoulder and learn something about the ground beneath my feet. I will go back out into the world buoyed by the knowledge that there are Black people on horseback fanning out over the streets of the city on any given day, and that our paths will cross again soon. And I will wait for those moments when, outside my window or in the park on a warm evening, I hear the unmistakable clip of an approaching horse's hooves against the asphalt. It is a sound that says to me, You are here. *You are here.*

ACKNOWLEDGMENTS

This book would not exist without the work, love, and commitment of people throughout the African diaspora who have ridden and taken care of horses for centuries. Thank you to the many named and unnamed ancestors whose lives animate this book.

Thank you to the waterways that have tended to me: the Atlantic Ocean, the Schuylkill River, the East River, the Hudson River, and the Caribbean Sea.

Thank you to my agent, Ayla Zuraw-Friedland, fellow Sagittarius and fiber artist, for believing in this book since its inception, and encouraging me to believe in myself. You have been the most steadfast, smart, and brilliant advocate a first-time author could hope for.

Thank you to my editor, Alexa Frank, fellow Sagittarius(!), for approaching our collaboration with insight and curiosity. You gave me the time and space to talk my shit, and for that I will be forever grateful. I'm so glad my manuscript found its way into the hands of a fellow Saddle Club lover. Thank you to the entire team at HarperCollins/Amistad who helped bring this book into being, including Yvonne Chan, Kyle O'Brien, Crissie Molina, Dawn Hall, and Abby West; a special thank-you to Sarah Kellogg for bringing my dream cover to life.

Thank you to Ica Sadagat for your fierce, generous, and bighearted editorial guidance. You have read (with, alongside) me with such great care. Salamat.

Thank you to Johanna Hedva for showing up for me across continents and time zones. Thank you for the voice messages, long emails, book recommendations, words of advice, the many years of chart readings, and the divinations.

Thank you to my parents for giving me life and believing in who I could be. Your love and labor continue to inform the work I do in the world.

Thank you to the editors who have supported me in sharing my work with readers, including Jessica Lynne at *Arts.Black*, Kaitlyn Greenidge at *Harper's Bazaar*, and Ha Duong at *Bomb* magazine.

Thank you to the educators whose thoughtfulness and rigor have shaped me as a thinker, including Jamie Green, Richard Blint, Debashree Mukherjee, Anelise Chen, and Natasha Lightfoot.

I would not be here, writing this today, without the deep and life-changing love of my friends.

ACKNOWLEDGMENTS

To Claire (fellow Sagittarius <3): Your knowledge and editorial eye have shaped this book since the beginning. Thank you for being a careful and willing first reader of this and many other texts, for a friendship that sustains and enlivens me, and for putting up with my bullshit.

Thank you to Janine for growing up alongside me and being a steadfast source of love, care, and gossip through countless transformations. I'm glad that I get to come home to you, no matter where in the world we are.

Sam, my watery babe and early-to-mid-2000s cultural literacy classmate—thank you for keeping me together, laughing and turning over ideas with me, and reminding me to stay curious.

Thank you, Deja, for the many processing sessions, dream interpretation voice notes, impromptu FaceTimes, Bike Yard dinner table hangouts, and for nourishing and cheering me on in so many ways.

Thank you, dear Maia, for the meandering conversations that expand my heart, and the breathwork/co-working hangs that helped me finish my manuscript draft.

The following people have provided invaluable support and friendship to me, anchoring me with small and large kindnesses and continual reminders that while the process of writing can be lonely, I am not in this alone. Many of them kept me company and kept me alive when I was recovering from a debilitating bike accident months before the final draft of my manuscript was due. I am a sharper thinker and a more honest, compassionate person because of them. Thank you to Wallace, Ireashia, Tita Nicky, Newt, Ira, Thao, Judy, Danya, Onion, Amirio, Yuan, Raine, Ace, Shze-Hui, Danialie, and Amirah.

Thank you to Billy.

Thank you to Zeba Blay and the members of the Spring 2023 Saturday writing circle.

Thank you to PB, Ducky, Keeper, Calmy, and the Wabie.

Lii, 我的愛人, thank you for meeting me in life and on the page with a practice of love that makes me feel so deeply held and cared for. Thank you for reminding me that the grief must be attended to, and thank you for your incisive, thorough edits on one of the essays I am most proud of in this book.

To the Bike Yard crew: Yilu, your big and generous visions have literally reshaped my life since 2020, leading me to new places and new friends, new understandings of what is possible when people come together in service and study—thank you. Thank you, Cris, for the thoughtful conversations, the reality TV show updates, the reggaeton Zumba workouts, and for modeling the kinds of faith, clarity, and integrity that I aspire to in my life. Thank you to everyone who has come through to a Thursday dinner and engaged in the vulnerable work of playing and learning together.

Kamal: my Leo, my love. Thank you for loving me with a

depth of patience and belief that has transformed the ways I see myself and others. Thank you for reminding me to trust in the wisdom of my voice and body. Thank you for fighting for me, and teaching me how to fight well.

Thank you to Jamie Figueroa and my Summer 2023 VONA cohort.

Thank you to the teachers and students of the School for Poetic Computation, particularly Melanie Hoff and Neta Bomani, for your brilliance, collaboration, and support.

Thank you to Diedrick Brackens for sharing the gift of your visionary weavings, and allowing your work to grace the cover of this book.

Thank you to my sister Ella, my first creative collaborator and co-conspirator. I am only a storyteller because of you.

WORKS CITED

INTRODUCTION

Castillo, Elaine. *How to Read Now: Essays*. Penguin, 2022.

NPR. "Serena Williams Wins Sportsperson of the Year; Poll Favored American Pharoah." December 14, 2015. https://www.npr.org/sections/thetwo-way/2015/12/14/459705249/.

FUGITIVITY

Authentic History of the English West Indies: With the Manners and Customs of the Free Inhabitants, Including Their Civil and Criminal Laws, Establishments, &c: A Description of the Climate, Buildings, Towns, & Sea Ports: With the Condition and Treatment. Ulan Press, 2012. Originally published in 1810.

Still, William. *The Underground Railroad Records: Narrating the Hardships, Hairbreadth Escapes, and Death Struggles of Slaves in Their Efforts for Freedom*. Modern Library, 2019.

Winer, Samantha. "North Carolina Runaway Slave Notices, 1750–1865." Digital Library on American Slavery, accessed January 27, 2025. https://dlas.uncg.edu/notices/history/.

COWBOY MYTHS

Alexander, Bryant Keith. "Writing/Righting Images of the West: A Brief Auto/Historiography of the Black Cowboy (Or 'I Want to Be a (Black) Cowboy' . . . Still)." *Cultural Studies ↔ Critical Methodologies* 14, no. 3 (2014): 227–31. https://doi.org/10.1177/1532708614527554.

Angermiller, Florence. "[Johanna July—Indian Woman Horsebreaker]: A Machine Readable Transcription." Library of Congress, uploaded 2015. www.loc.gov/resource/wpalh3.32061505/?st=gallery.

Austin, Stephen F. "The Texas Revolution." Digital History, uploaded 2021. Originally published in 1836. https://www.digitalhistory.uh.edu/disp_textbook.cfm?smtID=3&psid=554.

Benjamin, Nia, dir. high noon. Philadelphia Fringe Festival, September 18, 2022.

Boag, Peter. Re-Dressing America's Frontier Past. Univ. of California Press, 2011.

Bullock Museum. "Texas Rangers." Accessed January 27, 2025. https://www.thestoryoftexas.com/discover/campfire-stories/texas-ranger.

Castañeda, Antonia I. "Women of Color and the Rewriting of Western History: The Discourse, Politics, and Decolonization of History." Pacific Historical Review 61, no. 4 (1992): 501–33. https://doi.org/10.2307/3641046.

Gambino, Megan, and T. A. Frail. "Document Deep Dive: How the Homestead Act Transformed America." Smithsonian Magazine, May 2012. https://www.smithsonianmag.com/history/document-deep-dive-how-the-homestead-act-transformed-america-60005030/.

Hartman, Saidiya. Wayward Lives, Beautiful Experiments: Intimate Histories of Riotous Black Girls, Troublesome Women, and Queer Radicals. W. W. Norton, 2019.

"The Homestead Act of 1862." National Archives, accessed January 27, 2025. www.archives.gov/education/lessons/homestead-act.

Kelly, Donika. "Out West." In Bestiary: Poems. Graywolf Press, 2016.

Love, Nat. The Life and Adventures of Nat Love, Better Known in the Cattle Country as "Deadwood Dick," by Himself; a True History of Slavery Days, Life on the Great Cattle Ranges and on the Plains of the "Wild and Woolly" West, Based on Facts, and Personal Experiences of the Author. Documenting the American South, uploaded 1999. https://docsouth.unc.edu/neh/natlove/natlove.html.

National Park Service. "Native Americans and the Homestead Act." Accessed January 27, 2025. https://home.nps.gov/home/learn/historyculture/native-americans-and-the-homestead-act.htm.

Portée, Alexandria. "Danielle Deadwyler Defines Nineteenth Century Gender Norms in The Harder They Fall." Netflix Queue, November 26, 2021.

Samuel, Jeymes, dir. *The Harder They Fall*. Overbrook Entertainment, 2021.

Silverheels, Jay. Interview by Johnny Carson. *The Tonight Show*. NBC Entertainment, September 9, 1969.

Tayac, Gabrielle. *IndiVisible: African-Native American Lives in the Americas*. Smithsonian Books, 2009.

Wilder, Laura Ingalls. *Little House on the Prairie*. HarperCollins, 2016. Originally published in 1935.

DANCEHALL RODEO

Batson, Tanya. "When Cinemas Loomed Large." *Jamaica Gleaner*, March 24, 2002. http://old.jamaica-gleaner.com/gleaner/20020324/ent/ent1.html.

Black, Stephanie, dir. *Life and Debt*. New Yorker Films, 2001.

Brewster, Bill, and Frank Broughton. *Last Night a DJ Saved My Life*. Headline Book Publishing, 1999.

Chang, Jeff. *Can't Stop Won't Stop: A History of the Hip-Hop Generation*. Picador, 2005.

Lesser, Beth. *Dancehall: The Rise of Jamaican Dancehall Culture*. Soul Jazz Books, 2023.

Lone Ranger. *Hi-Yo, Silver, Away!* Greensleeves Records, 1982.

Stolzoff, Norman C. *Wake the Town and Tell the People: Dancehall Culture in Jamaica*. Duke Univ. Press, 2000.

Williams, Stereo. "'90s Hip-Hop's Love Affair with Dancehall." *Rock the Bells*, uploaded May 31, 2021.

PONY BOOKS

Abate, Michelle Ann. *Tomboys: A Literary and Cultural History*. Temple Univ. Press, 2008.

Avery, Gillian. *Behold the Child: American Children and Their Books, 1621–1922*. Johns Hopkins Univ. Press, 1994.

Badger, Jane. *Heroines on Horseback: The Pony Book in Children's Fiction*. Girls Gone By Publishers, 2013.

Bagnold, Enid. *National Velvet*. Heinemann, 1935.

Bibby, Miriam A. "Not Just for Girls: The Past—and Future—of the Pony Book." *Historyonhorseback*, August 7, 2013. https://historyonhorse back.com/2013/08/07/not-just-for-girls-the-past-and-future-of-the -pony-book/.

Brand, Dionne. "Arriving at Desire." In *Desire in Seven Voices*, edited by Lorna Crozier. Douglas & McIntyre, 1999.

Brooke, Lauren. *Coming Home (Heartland #1)*. Scholastic Paperbacks, 2000.

Brooke, Lauren. *The New Class (Chestnut Hill #1)*. Scholastic Paperbacks, 2005.

Brown, Amy. "Girls Galloping Horses: Unstable Identities." *New Zealand Review of Books*, September 11, 2018.

Bryant, Bonnie. *Horse Crazy (Saddle Club #1)*. Gareth Stevens Publishing, 1995.

Campbell, Joanna. *A Horse Called Wonder (Thoroughbred #1)*. HarperCollins, 1991.

Harrison, Barbara, and Gregory Maguire, eds. *Innocence and Experience: Essays and Conversations on Children's Literature*. Lothrop, Lee and Shepard, 1987.

Jane Badger Books. "The Pony Book in WWII: Part 1." *The Pony Book Encyclopedia*, August 16, 2024. https://janebadgerbooks.co.uk/the-pony-book-in-wwii-part-1/.

Jones, Stephanie. "Grass Houses: Representations and Reinventions of Social Class through Children's Literature." *Journal of Language and Literacy Education* 4, no. 2 (2008): 40–58. https://files.eric.ed.gov/fulltext/EJ1068167.pdf.

Kendrick, Jenny. "Riders, Readers, Romance: A Short History of the Pony Story." *Jeunesse: Young People, Texts, Cultures* 1, no. 2 (2009): 183–202. https://dx.doi.org/10.1353/jeu.2010.0012.

Lerer, Seth. *Children's Literature: A Reader's History, from Aesop to Harry Potter*. Univ. of Chicago Press, 2009.

Mickenberg, Julia L. *Learning from the Left: Children's Literature, the Cold War, and Radical Politics in the United States*. Oxford Univ. Press, 2005.

O'Malley, Andrew. *The Making of the Modern Child: Children's Literature in the Late Eighteenth Century*. Children's Literature and Culture. Routledge, 2003.

Sewell, Anna. *Black Beauty*. Jarrold & Sons, 1877.

NOTHING WITHOUT EACH OTHER

Castillo, Elaine. *How to Read Now: Essays*. Penguin, 2022.

Custo, Arnie, dir. *The Saddle Club*. Season 2, episode 1, "A Horse of a Different Colour: Part 1." Crawfords Australia, Protocol Entertainment, 2003.

Custo, Arnie, dir. *The Saddle Club*. Season 2, episode 2, "A Horse of a Different Colour: Part 2." Crawfords Australia, Protocol Entertainment, 2003.

Defriest, Mark, dir. *The Saddle Club*. Season 2, episode 25, "Horse's Keeper." Crawfords Australia, Protocol Entertainment, 2003.

Haraway, Donna J. *Modest_Witness@Second_Millennium. FemaleMan _Meets_OncoMouse: Feminism and Technoscience*. Routledge, 1997.

Sharp, Peter, dir. *The Saddle Club*. Season 1, episode 15, "Gift Horse." Crawfords Australia, Protocol Entertainment, 2001.

HORSE OF THE DIVINE

Apollo. "Shrine of the Times—A Yoruba Masterpiece in Focus." *Apollo*, June 21, 2022.

Beckwith, Martha Warren. *Black Roadways: A Study of Jamaica Folk Life*. Negro Univ. Press, 1969. Originally published by Univ. of North Carolina Press, 1929.

Beier, Ulli, comp. and ed. *Yoruba Poetry: An Anthology of Traditional Poems*. Cambridge Univ. Press, 1970.

Brown, Vincent. "Spiritual Terror and Sacred Authority in Jamaican Slave Society." *Slavery & Abolition* 24, no. 1 (2003): 24–53. https://doi.org/10.1080/714005263.

"*Figure of Shango on Horseback*: Yorùbá, Toibo of Erin." Brooklyn Museum, accessed January 27, 2025. https://www.brooklynmuseum.org/opencollection/objects/4951.

Hurston, Zora Neale. *Tell My Horse: Voodoo and Life in Haiti and Jamaica*. Harper Perennial, 1938.

Hyacinthe, Genevieve. "Tiona Nekkia McClodden and Genevieve Hyacinthe on Black Atlantic Religion and Contemporary Art." *Art in America*, February 1, 2021. https://www.artnews.com/art-in-america/interviews/black-atlantic-religion-contemporary-art-1234582628/.

McEwen, Abigail. *Revolutionary Horizons: Art and Polemics in 1950s Cuba*. Yale Univ. Press, 2016.

Noël, Samantha A. "The Embodiment of the *Femme Cheval* in Wifredo Lam's *Je Suis*." *Latin American and Latinx Visual Culture* 6, no. 1 (2024): 122–26. https://doi.org/10.1525/lavc.2024.6.1.122.

Pemberton, John, III, ed. *Insight and Artistry in African Divination*. Smithsonian Institution Press, 2000.

Sato, Paula. "Wifredo Lam, the Shango Priestess, and the Femme Che-val." *Journal of International Women's Studies* 17, no. 3 (2016): article 8. https://vc.bridgew.edu/jiws/vol17/iss3/8.

Sims, Lowery Stokes. *Wifredo Lam and the International Avant-Garde, 1923–1982*. Univ. of Texas Press, 2002.

Tortello, Rebecca. "The Fall of a Gentle Giant: The Collapse of Tom Cringle's Cotton Tree." Pieces of the Past, *Jamaica Gleaner*, accessed January 27, 2025. https://old.jamaica-gleaner.com/pages/history/story0020.html.

Velasco, David. "1000 Words: Tiona Nekkia McClodden." *Artforum*, May 2019. https://www.artforum.com/features/tiona-nekkia-mcclodden-talks-about-i-prayed-to-the-wrong-god-for-you-243130/.

BECOMING ANIMAL

Belcourt, Billy-Ray, George Dust, and Kay Gabriel. "Top or Bottom: How Do We Desire?" *The New Inquiry*, October 10, 2018. https://thenewinquiry.com/top-or-bottom-how-do-we-desire/.

Cruz, Ariane. *The Color of Kink: Black Women, BDSM, and Pornography*. New York Univ. Press, 2016.

WORKING ANIMALS

Burnard, Trevor. "A New Look at the Zong Case of 1783." *XVII–XVIII: Revue de la Société d'Études Anglo-Américaines des XVIIe et XVIIIe Siècles* 76 (2019). https://doi.org/10.4000/1718.1808.

Crucchiola, Jordan. "Boots Riley Tells Us the Story Behind *Sorry to Bother You*'s Horse People." *Vulture*, February 4, 2019. https://www.vulture.com/2019/02/oscars-2019-the-birth-of-sorry-to-bother-yous-horse-people.html.

Douglass, Frederick. "Agriculture and Black Progress: An Address Delivered in Nashville, Tennessee, on September 18, 1873." The Frederick Douglass Papers Project, accessed January 27, 2025, https://frederickdouglasspapersproject.com/s/digitaledition/item/17769.

Douglass, Frederick. *Narrative of the Life of Frederick Douglass, an American Slave*. Gildan Media, 2019.

Grundy, David. "Horses and History." *Social Text Online*, June 30, 2020. https://socialtextjournal.org/periscope_article/horses-and-history/.

Jackson, Zakiyyah Iman. "Losing Manhood: Animality and Plasticity in the (Neo)Slave Narrative." *Qui Parle* 25, no. 1–2 (2016): 95–136. https://doi.org/10.5250/quiparle.25.1-2.0095.

Johnson, Walter. *River of Dark Dreams: Slavery and Empire in the Cotton Kingdom*. Harvard Univ. Press, 2017.

Philip, M. NourbeSe. *Zong!* Wesleyan Univ. Press, 2008.

Riley, Boots, dir. *Sorry to Bother You*. Annapurna Pictures, 2018.

EQUESTRIAN CHIC

"1986 Polo by Ralph Lauren 'It's a tradition, a way of life' TV Commercial." YouTube, uploaded by ewjxn, May 3, 2021. https://www.youtube.com/watch?v=-4GTRfPJS_I.

Adler, Dan. "The History of Hip-Hop's Obsession with Polo Ralph Lauren." *Esquire*, August 16, 2016. https://www.esquire.com/style/a47568/hip-hop-polo-ralph-lauren-history/.

Backman, Melvin. "Polo Ralph Lauren's Complicated Streetwear Past." *New Yorker*, February 2, 2018. https://www.newyorker.com/culture/culture-desk/polo-ralph-laurens-complicated-streetwear-past.

Belinky, Biju. "Inside the Slick, Stylish World of Black Dandyism." *Huck*, July 21, 2017. https://www.huckmag.com/article/black-dandyism.

Cowen, Trace William. "North West Recreates Classic Kanye West Polo Fit from 2004." *Complex*, August 23, 2023. https://www.complex.com/style/a/tracewilliamcowen/north-west-recreates-kanye-west-polo-outfit.

"Fashion Bomber of the Day: Jidenna from Brooklyn + Behind the Scenes of Classic Man." *Fashion Bomb Daily*, April 17, 2015. https://fashionbombdaily.com/2015/04/17/fashion-bomber-of-the-day-jidenna-from-brooklyn-behind-the-scenes-of-classic-man/.

Fitzgerald, Adam. "An Interview with Fred Moten, Part 1." *Lit Hub*, August 5, 2015. https://lithub.com/an-interview-with-fred-moten-pt-i/.

Gander, Kashmira. "Bows and Brogues: Why Female Black Dandies Are the Ultimate Rebels." *Independent*, September 5, 2016. https://www.the-independent.com/life-style/fashion/black-dandies-women-rebel-dandy-lion-project-brighton-photo-biennale-jay-z-kanye-africa-boateng-brazzaville-a7218431.html.

Gill-Peterson, Jules. "The Un-Importance of Wearing Clothes." *Sad Brown Girl*, Substack, March 6, 2024. https://sadbrowngirl.substack.com/p/the-un-importance-of-wearing-clothes.

High, Kemet. "The Real and Raucous Story of the Lo Life Crew." *Fader*, December 7, 2016. https://www.thefader.com/2016/12/07/lo-life-crew-interview.

Howl, Thirstin, III, and Tom Gould. *Bury Me with the Lo On*. Victory Editions, 2017.

Hsu, Hua. "The Brooklyn Street Crews That Boosted Ralph Lauren and Invented Their Own Style." *New Yorker*, July 8, 2016. https://www.newyorker.com/culture/photo-booth/the-brooklyn-street-crews-who-boosted-ralph-lauren-and-invented-their-own-style.

Miller, Monica L. *Slaves to Fashion: Black Dandyism and the Styling of Black Diasporic Identity*. Duke Univ. Press, 2009.

Monáe, Janelle. Interview with *Access Hollywood*. Posted September 9, 2019, by *Access Hollywood*. https://www.youtube.com/watch?v=gA1S4ngG-xc.

Scobie, Edward. *Black Britannia: A History of Blacks in Britain*. Johnson Publishing, 1972.

Tsjeng, Zing. "The Incredibly Dressed 'Lady Dandies' of the Congo Are Here to Ruin You." *Vice*, September 29, 2017. https://www.vice.com/en/article/the-incredibly-dressed-lady-dandies-of-the-congo-are-here-to-ruin-you/.

Vice TV. "Meeting the Crew Who Reshaped NYC Fashion | Black Market." YouTube, uploaded by Vice TV, May 17, 2022. https://youtube/AGia7ui1Eg0?si=xUtc3flR5R6uqGhW.

White, Shane, and Graham White. *Stylin': African-American Expressive Culture from Its Beginnings to the Zoot Suit*. Cornell Univ. Press, 1999.

XXL Staff. "Polo and Hip-Hop, An Oral History [Pt. 1]." *XXL*, November 30, 2010. https://www.xxlmag.com/polo-and-hip-hop-an-oral-history-pt-1/.

COWBOY CARTER

Berger, John. "Some Notes on Song: The Rhythms of Listening." *Harper's Magazine*, February 2015. https://harpers.org/archive/2015/02/some-notes-on-song/.

Beyoncé. "Beyoncé—Run the World (Girls) (Official Video)." YouTube, uploaded by Beyoncé, May 18, 2011. https://www.youtube.com/watch?v=VBmMU_iwe6U.

Beyoncé. *Cowboy Carter.* Parkwood Entertainment and Columbia Records, March 29, 2024.

Beyoncé. "Daddy Lessons." On *Lemonade.* Parkwood Entertainment and Columbia Records, April 23, 2016.

"Beyoncé Performing at the Houston Livestock Show and Rodeo | 2004." YouTube, uploaded by Vault Of Beyoncé, May 3, 2023. https://www.youtube.com/watch?v=WzEo15Zm6uA.

Cabrera, Kristen. "Tucked Away for 40 Years, These Juneteenth Rodeo Photos Ride Once More." *Texas Standard,* June 19, 2024. https://www.texasstandard.org/stories/juneteenth-rodeo-book-sarah-bird-photos-texas-black-cowboys/.

Israel (@Israel). "@Beyonce there's a little girl named Emily who's been through a lot and would love to meet you." Twitter (now X), December 2, 2023, 12:52 p.m. https://x.com/Israel/status/1731008559737934190.

Lil Nas X. "Lil Nas X—Old Town Road (Official Movie) ft. Billy Ray Cyrus," YouTube, uploaded by Lil Nas X, May 17, 2019. https://www.youtube.com/watch?v=w2Ov5jzm3j8.

Mehri, Momtaza. "On Pleasure & Power(lessness)." *bywayofnoway,* Substack, March 31, 2024. https://bynoway.substack.com/p/black-feminist-transference-on-pleasure.

Morris, Woody. "Palestinian Horse Centre Vows to Rebuild after West Bank Demolition." BBC, August 11, 2024. www.bbc.com/news/articles/cy68g5zz1wjo.

Pecknold, Diane. *Hidden in the Mix: The African American Presence in Country Music.* Duke Univ. Press, 2013.

Schonfeld, Zach. "'We Were a Part of History': Beyoncé and the Chicks' Audacious CMAs Set, and the Volatile Reaction Offstage, as Told by Its Background Performers." *Vulture,* March 27, 2024. https://www.vulture.com/article/beyonce-cmas-the-chicks-oral-history.html.

Wallace, Christian. "Myrtis Dightman Is the Jackie Robinson of Rodeo." *Texas Monthly,* February 2023. https://www.texasmonthly.com/arts-entertainment/myrtis-dightman-rodeo-cowboy/.

Wisniewska, Zuzanna. "Southwestern Colored Cowboys Association (1940s–1950s)." *Blackpast*, January 27, 2018. www.blackpast.org/african-american-history/southwestern-colored-cowboys-association-1940s-1950s/.

WHEN NO SOFTNESS CAME

Golden, Mark. *Sport and Society in Ancient Greece*. Cambridge Univ. Press, 1998.

Gumbs, Alexis Pauline. *Dub: Finding Ceremony*. Duke Univ. Press, 2020.

Odell, Jenny. *Saving Time: Discovering a Life Beyond the Clock*. Random House, 2023.

Quashie, Kevin. *The Sovereignty of Quiet*. Rutgers Univ. Press, July 25, 2012.

Shang, Ntozake. *Sassafrass, Cypress & Indigo: A Novel*. St. Martin's Griffin, 2010.

Sosa, Mercedes. "Duerme, Negrito." On *El grito de la tierra*. Philips, 1970.

AFTER THE CAMERAS

Bevins, Vincent. *If We Burn: The Mass Protest Decade and the Missing Revolution*. PublicAffairs, 2023.

Cachero, Paulina. "The True Story of the Black Cowboys of Philadelphia Depicted in *Concrete Cowboy*." *Time*, April 2, 2021. https://time.com/5952050/concrete-cowboy-true-story-netflix/.

Duran, Mariana. "Horseback Riders Celebrate 'Equestrian Lifestyle' in San Gabriel Valley. Can It Survive?" *Los Angeles Times*, June 26, 2023. https://www.latimes.com/california/story/2023-06-26/horseback-riders-celebrate-equestrian-lifestyle-in-san-gabriel-valley-can-it-survive.

Kaur, Harmeet, and Melissa Alonso. "A Black Man Who Was Led Through Galveston, Texas, by Police Officers on Horseback Is Suing the City for $1 Million." *CNN*, October 12, 2020. https://www.cnn.com/2020/10/12/us/galveston-horseback-arrest-lawsuit-trnd/index.html.

Lauer, Alex. "A Short History of Americans Riding Horses into Protests." *Insidehook*, June 10, 2020. https://www.insidehook.com/culture/history-americans-riding-horses-protests.

Manthey, Grace, Frank Esposito, and Amanda Hernandez. "Despite 'Defunding' Claims, Police Funding Has Increased in Many US Cities."

ABC News, October 16, 2022. https://abcnews.go.com/US/defunding-claims-police-funding-increased-us-cities/story?id=91511971.

Rodriguez, Jo Fitzgerald. "Oakland's Protest Rider on Why She Took to Horseback for George Floyd." KQED, June 2, 2020. https://www.kqed.org/news/11822227/oaklands-protest-rider-on-why-she-took-to-horseback-for-george-floyd.

Scott-Reid, Jessica. "At Black Lives Matter Protests, Police Horses Become Another Troubling Symbol of Oppression." *Sentient Media*, June 25, 2020. https://sentientmedia.org/black-lives-matter-protests-police-horses-oppression/.

Selvin, Claire, and Tess Solomon. "Toppled and Removed Monuments: A Continually Updated Guide to Statues and the Black Lives Matter Protests." *ARTnews*, June 11, 2020. www.artnews.com/art-news/news/monuments-black-lives-matter-guide-1202690845/.

ABOUT THE AUTHOR

Bitter Kalli was born and raised in Brooklyn, New York. Their essays and criticism have been published in *Harper's Bazaar*, *Architectural Digest*, and *Bomb* magazines, among others. They are a landworker and the founder of Star Apple Nursery, a project focused on the stewardship of Caribbean and Southeast Asian heritage crops. Bitter is a child of the Atlantic Ocean. They are based in Philadelphia.